SCOTLAND'S CANALS

Oh! The Crinan Canal for me,
I don't like the wild raging sea,
The big foaming breakers
would give me the shakers,
The Crinan Canal for me.

Chorus from
The Crinan Canal for me

Scotland's Canals

NICK HAYNES

HISTORIC SCOTLAND
in association with
SCOTTISH CANALS

Edinburgh 2015

Published by Historic Scotland
Longmore House · Salisbury Place
Edinburgh EH91SH

Text © Historic Scotland and the author

Nick Haynes asserts the moral rights to be identified
as the author of this work

ISBN 978 1 84917 165 6

Front cover: The Kelpies at Helix Park
photograph by Peter Sandground

Back cover: The Falkirk Wheel
photograph by Nick Haynes

Frontispiece: Avon Aqueduct
photograph by Peter Sandground

Designed and typeset in Sweet Sans by Dalrymple
Printed on Condat Matt 150gsm and bound by
Albe de Coker, Antwerp

www.historic-scotland.gov.uk
www.scottishcanals.co.uk

If you have enjoyed this book, you may like *Scotland*'s
First World War and *Scotland*'s *Sporting Buildings*.
Both titles are published by Historic Scotland.

For Sara and Simon

The author is particularly grateful to Elizabeth McCrone
of Historic Scotland and Cara Baillie of Scottish
Canals for their enthusiastic commitment to this
project, and would also like to thank for their support
and expertise: Janis Adams; Neil Adams (RCAHMS);
Michelle Andersson (HS); Stuart Baird; Gordon Barr;
Sandy Bell; Rachael Egan (Archives, GU); Richard
Emerson; Lydia Fisher (RCAHMS); Andrew Fleming;
Karen Gallagher (CultureNL Ltd.); Norman Gray;
Lynsey Halliday (NLS); Miriam McDonald (RCAHMS);
Ranald MacInnes (HS); Finlay Martin (HS); Gordon
Masterton (Vice Chairman, RCAHMS); Chris O'Connell
(SC); Lesley Richmond (Deputy Director University
Library and University Archivist, GU); Nicola Russell
(GU); Peter Sandground; Clare Sorensen (RCAHMS);
Vanessa Stephen; and Emma Yan (GU).
NH

GU University of Glasgow
HS Historic Scotland
NLS National Library of Scotland
RCAHMS Royal Commission on the Ancient &
Historical Monuments of Scotland
SC Scottish Canals

Scottish
Canals

HISTORIC SCOTLAND
ALBA AOSMHOR

Preface

This book is a general introduction to the built heritage of Scotland's five surviving canals: the Forth and Clyde; the Monkland; the Crinan; the Caledonian; and the Union. The genesis of the book lies in a collaborative project between Historic Scotland and Scottish Canals to survey and update the listed building records for Scottish Canals' large and varied historic estate. The results of the survey have now been incorporated into the list of buildings of special architectural or historic interest, which can be accessed via Historic Scotland's website: www.historic-scotland.gov.uk. The canal trenches themselves and many of their associated structures are scheduled monuments, details of which are also available on Historic Scotland's website. The revised lists and the schedules form important components in Scottish Canals' planning for the maintenance, repair, management and development of these extraordinary monuments of the early Industrial Age.

The chapters are arranged in date order of construction of the major surviving canals. The introduction aims to set out the broad context in which the canals came to be built and developed. The focus of the text is on the engineering achievements of the canal-builders. As a primer on the subject, the book can only touch on the complex social, economic, cultural and environmental histories of Scotland's canals, which are told in more detail elsewhere.

For the purposes of consistency, Imperial measurements are given throughout the text, as this was the measurement system used for the construction of the canals.

Overview

Canals for irrigation, water supply, garden ornament and hydropower have long and fascinating histories, as do canalised rivers (rivers artificially deepened for navigation), but it is the development of freestanding navigable canals in Scotland that forms the focus of this book.

Three of the five surviving Scottish canals, the Forth and Clyde, Crinan and Caledonian, are 'summit level' ship canals. These link tidal rivers or sea lochs via routes that rise to plateaus between valleys and return to sea level. The primary purpose of these canals was through-trade, reducing otherwise circuitous and dangerous sea routes. The remaining two extant canals, the Union and the Monkland, are 'level line' or 'contour' inland canals, which have no changes in level and do not connect directly to rivers or the sea. Both canals were established for the main purpose of transporting coal to the big cities in order to break existing monopolies on fuel supply (and in consequence to reduce the price). The different purposes of the canals determined their characteristics: the summit level canals are deeper and have locks and swing or lifting bridges to accommodate ocean-going sailing vessels of the period; the contour canals are more circuitous to avoid the expensive construction of locks as far as possible, and they are shallow with fixed masonry bridges that were suitable only for shallow barges pulled by horses. Both the Crinan and Caledonian Canals have remained in operation since their construction, while the Forth and Clyde and Union Canals were officially abandoned in the 1960s before being resuscitated for leisure and amenity purposes in 2000. The Monkland Canal was abandoned in 1950 and the open water much reduced by the construction of the M8 motorway and infilling of the section through Coatbridge.

Although other canals were built in Scotland in the late eighteenth and early nineteenth centuries, and many more were planned, the country's topography, dispersed population centres and existing maritime trading routes mitigated against an extensive canal network. With the exception of the Caledonian Canal, which was always a state-funded project, the country's canals all began life as commercial ventures and ended up as national assets.

The Scottish canal mania lasted a relatively short time, from the start of the Forth and Clyde Canal in 1768 until the completion of the Edinburgh and Glasgow Railway in 1842. Even as the last major canal, the Caledonian, was under construction, the rapid development of steam power threatened the viability of the canals. New steamboats were larger, faster and more powerful than their predecessors, with potential to damage the infrastructure of the canals and the ability to voyage in difficult seas avoiding canal dues (tolls). The speed, convenience and flexibility of the railway network had an immediate and savage impact on the always-fragile profitability of the canals. From the 1840s onwards, rival railway companies purchased a number of the canal companies, and some filled in the routes and laid them with railway tracks. Other canals continued operating in railway company ownership, but in all cases the traffic and revenues declined dramatically as the nineteenth century progressed and the railway network grew. The canals were too small for modern waterborne traffic, too inflexible in their construction and operation, too expensive to maintain, and lacked a properly integrated network. Towards the end of the nineteenth century and throughout the twentieth century, the old canal infrastructure of narrow, steep and weak bridges or low aqueducts placed restrictions on the burgeoning road network.

In the face of competition from the railways the commercial trade on the canals had largely ceased by the end of the First World War, leaving the neglected Lowland canals in a state of near-dereliction. The Caledonian Canal and the Crinan Canal remained in operation, but were transferred to the Ministry of Transport under an Act of 1919. Some investment took place between the wars in repairs and new bridges capable of carrying motor traffic, but the new mechanised swing bridges still required staff to operate them and caused traffic delays.

The crowning glory of the Maryhill Burgh Halls was
a series of twenty stained glass windows made by
the Glasgow firm of Stephen Adam. These windows
commemorate the industries of Maryhill, and the men
and women who worked in them.

**Map of Scotland Showing the Five Existing
Scottish Canals**

The general dilapidation of the UK's waterways
prompted the formation of the Inland Waterways
Association in 1946 to campaign for their improvement. The Transport Act of 1947 came into force on
1 January 1948, nationalising the remaining canals
along with the railways, buses and ports under
the authority of the British Transport Commission.
Pressure to formally abandon the Lowland canals
grew as some, notably the Monkland Canal and
the Glasgow branch of the Forth and Clyde Canal,
attracted a shocking level of accidents and
appeared to constrain new development in old
industrial centres.[1] A Board of Survey covering
British Transport Commission waterways was
set up in 1954 under the chairmanship of Lord
Rusholme. The board's report formed the basis
for the 1958 (Leslie) Bowes Committee of Inquiry
into Inland Waterways, which recommended the
retention of the Caledonian and Crinan Canals as a
'social service' and closure of the Forth and Clyde
and Union Canals.[2]

Four years later the British Transport
Commission was abolished and a new organisation,
the British Waterways Board, was given responsibility to manage Scotland's canals with 'due regard
to efficiency, economy and safety of operation
and, secondly, to review the whole problem of
waterways which are no longer self-supporting and
to formulate proposals with the object of putting
these waterways to the best use'. In the case of the
Monkland Canal, it was determined that its best
use would be infilling and redevelopment as part of
Scotland's motorway network. The Glasgow Branch
of the Forth and Cylde Canal also came under threat
of infilling for the Maryhill motorway.[3]

However, by the time of the Transport Act of
1968, there was a recognition that canals had
amenity and recreational values, and also that
infilling was substantially more expensive than
repairing. By 1970 only the Crinan and Caledonian
Canals remained in use, classified as 'cruising
waterways'. Almost as soon as the Forth and Clyde,
Union and Monkland Canals closed, pressure had
grown to revitalise these 'remainder waterways'

as amenity assets for local communities. From
1976 no further obstructions were allowed to the
surviving stretches of canal, and regular clean-ups
were organised. In 1986 there was the first major
project to reopen a stretch of the Forth and Clyde
Canal from Temple to Kirkintilloch. Increasingly,
the ecological and environmental importance of
the canals as integral parts of the country's water
management system came to be recognised during
the 1980s.

With the advent of the National Lottery in 1994
the opportunity arose to refurbish and reopen
both the Forth and Clyde and Union Canals by
means of the Millennium Link Project. The project
reawakened public interest in the canals, and has
led to a renaissance of the network. Following the
approval of the British Waterways Board (Transfer
of Functions) Order 2012, Scottish Canals assumed
responsibility for canals in Scotland.

At the time of writing, feasibility studies are
underway for a five-mile Lomond Canal from the
southern end of Loch Lomond through Alexandria
and the Vale of Leven to the River Clyde at
Dumbarton. The prime function of the canal is
intended to be flood mitigation and water management, but it would also serve as a stimulus to regeneration. The Lomond Canal would be Scotland's
first new canal in almost 200 years.

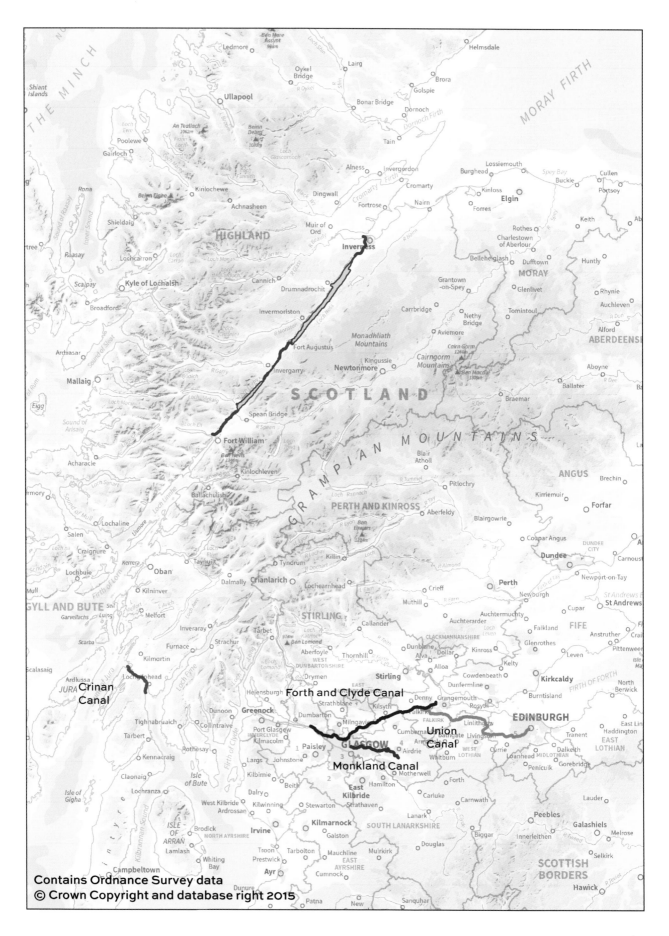

Crinan Canal

Forth and Clyde Canal

Union Canal

Monkland Canal

Contains Ordnance Survey data
© Crown Copyright and database right 2015

Forth and Clyde Canal

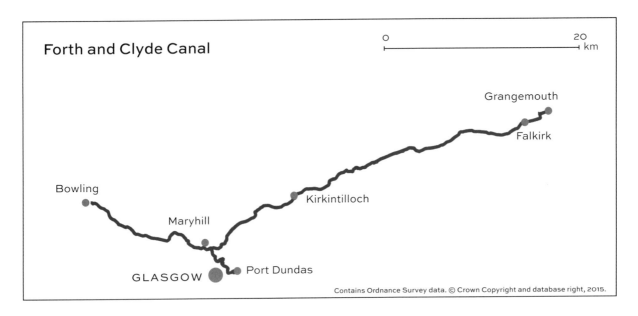

Contains Ordnance Survey data. © Crown Copyright and database right, 2015.

Monkland Canal

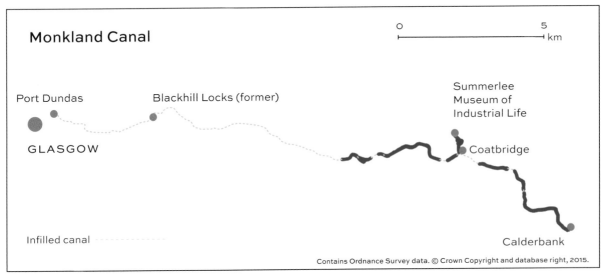

Infilled canal ----------

Contains Ordnance Survey data. © Crown Copyright and database right, 2015.

Union Canal

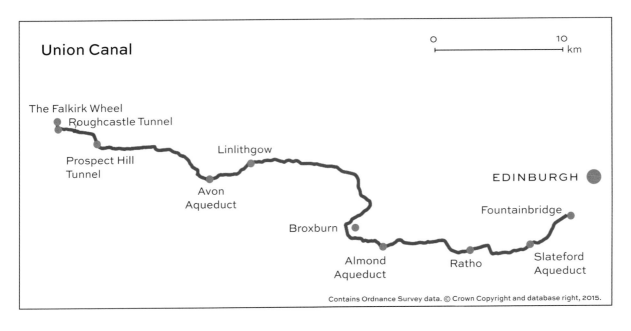

Contains Ordnance Survey data. © Crown Copyright and database right, 2015.

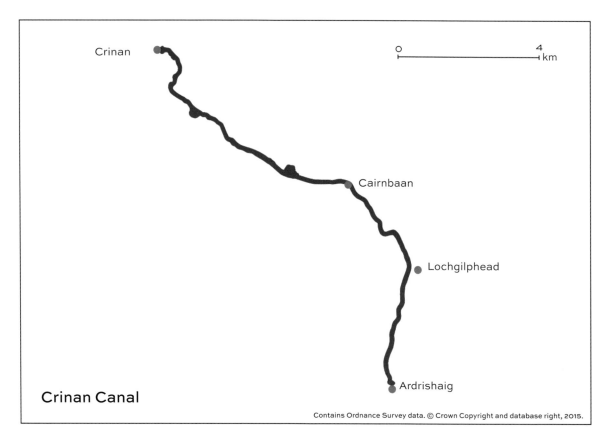

Crinan Canal

Crinan

Cairnbaan

Lochgilphead

Ardrishaig

0 — 4 km

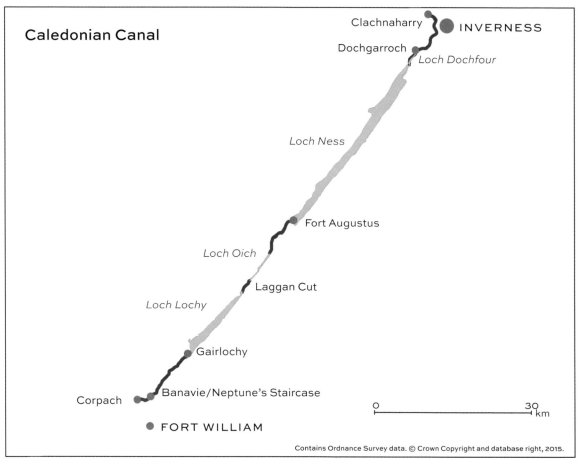

Caledonian Canal

Clachnaharry

INVERNESS

Dochgarroch

Loch Dochfour

Loch Ness

Fort Augustus

Loch Oich

Laggan Cut

Loch Lochy

Gairlochy

Corpach

Banavie/Neptune's Staircase

FORT WILLIAM

0 — 30 km

Introduction

The Grand Canal, China
IStock

Here at Wuxi in Jiangsu Province, agriculture and the silk industry flourished after the construction of the canal. The Grand Canal of China is still the longest navigable canal in the world and stretches over 1,100 miles from Beijing to Hangzhou. It is a UNESCO World Heritage site.

A BRIEF HISTORY OF EARLY INTERNATIONAL CANALS

The world history of canal-building for navigation is ancient. Aristotle's *Meteorology* identifies Sesostris, a pharaoh of Egypt in the second millennium BCE (Before Common Era), as the first to attempt a ship canal linking the River Nile to the Red Sea. It is not clear if or how far this great project progressed, but a canal through the Wadi Tumilat does appear to have been dug during the reign of the Egyptian pharaoh, Necho II, and extended or re-excavated by the Persian emperor, Darius I, in the sixth and the fifth centuries BCE.[1] Work on the 'Hong Gou', or 'Canal of the Flying Geese', linking the Yellow River to the Si and Bian Rivers is also thought to have begun in the sixth century BCE (Before Common Era). In the seventh century CE (Common Era) this was to become incorporated as part of the world's longest canal, the Grand Canal of China, which still stretches over 1,100 miles from Beijing to Hangzhou. Although ancient civilisations possessed technology for moving vessels between different water levels, it appears to have been relatively rudimentary: either dragging boats across inclined planes between levels; or using 'flash locks' that comprised single gates opened to discharge both water and vessels in a torrent; or for boats to be winched upstream. Both the Ancient Greeks and Romans planned and built substantial canals for navigation, but their use of the now familiar 'pound locks', in which two sets of gates enclose a regulating basin, is disputed.

Canal-building for transport was revived in the medieval period, notably in China, the Low Countries, Germany and Italy. The earliest European prototype of a modern pound lock was constructed at Vreeswijk in the Netherlands in 1373. Bertola da Novate is thought to have introduced the first 'mitre' gates, pairs of gates that work with the water pressure and meet together in a shallow V-shape, in Italy in the mid-fifteenth century (replacing the old 'portcullis' or 'guillotine' gates that restricted headroom). Leonardo da Vinci, the outstanding European scientist, inventor and artist

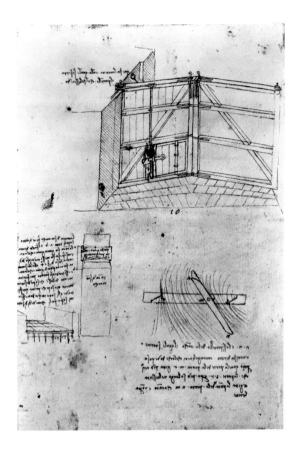

This sketch taken from a notebook by Leonardo da Vinci shows his invention for a low-level hatch in the gates that allows control over the water into the lock. Da Vinci was the most outstanding Italian painter, sculptor, architect and engineer of the Renaissance period. He had a wide knowledge of the sciences, including biology, anatomy, physiology, hydro-dynamics, mechanics and aeronautics. His notebooks, written in mirror writing, contain original remarks on all of these areas.

(later incorporated into the Canal du Midi) under the patronage of Louis XIV and his minister of finance, Jean-Baptiste Colbert, to link Toulouse to the Mediterranean. As well as their practical transport purposes, such schemes were demonstrations of political and economic power and technical inge-nuity, and expressions of national confidence and pride. King Charles II planned his own grand canal project in Scotland to link the River Clyde and the River Forth, but the estimated £500,000 costs ensured that the scheme never progressed in his lifetime.[6]

SCOTTISH CONTEXT IN THE EIGHTEENTH CENTURY

In spite of the development of turnpike (toll) roads from 1713 and the four Highland military roads from 1725, Scotland's transport infrastructure remained in a generally dilapidated state, described vividly in the 1824 supplement to the *Encyclopaedia Britannica*:

Until after the middle of last century there was scarcely any thing that deserved the name of a good road in Scotland. About the year 1732, indeed, Government began to open up the country by road made by the military, hence called Military Roads, which extended in all about 800 miles; but these being confined for the most part to the Highlands, and intended only for military purposes, and formed with little or no regard to such ascents and descents as do not impede the passage of an army, were of little advantage to the more populous parts of the country. It is within the recollection of persons still alive, when corn, coals, and other heavy articles, were usually carried on the backs of horses, even in the southern counties of Scotland; the roads or rather the tracks being for the greater part of the year unfit for wheel-carriages.[7]

The benefits of efficient transport to trade, industry and agriculture were clear to the improving land-owners and entrepreneurs of early eighteenth-century Scotland, but the political and financial circumstances were lacking. Such canals as were

of the late fifteenth and early sixteenth centuries, took a great interest in practical hydraulics and lock technology, developing a low-level hatch in the lock-gates that allowed a controlled influx of water without swamping the boats.[2]

The reputed remains of Scotland's first navigable canal can be seen behind the old manse at Largo in Fife, where in about 1495 the renowned admiral Sir Andrew Wood is believed to have constructed a level canal 'From his house, down almost as far as the church ... upon which he used to sail in his barge to the church every Sunday in great state'.[3] Doubt was cast on the story by excavation of part of the site in 1992, which failed to find evidence of the puddle clay necessary to retain the trench as a water-filled canal.[4] No other navigational canals are recorded in the country until the eighteenth century.

By the seventeenth century the construc-tion of canals on a truly grand scale had spread across Europe from France in the west to Russia in the east. The first summit level canal to cross a watershed using pound locks was the Briare Canal of 1604–42, linking the Loire and Seine river systems via forty-one locks.[5] The grandest of the grand schemes was undoubtedly that of Pierre-Paul Riquet, Baron de Bonrepos, and the surveyor François Andréossy, who from 1666 to 1681 constructed the Canal royal en Languedoc

Blackhall Aqueduct, Paisley
Nick Haynes

This is the longest single span masonry aqueduct of the canal age and the oldest surviving viaduct in use for an active railway in the UK. The Blackhall Aqueduct was designed under Thomas Telford as a single span of eighty-eight feet and six inches, and constructed over the White Cart Water in 1808–10. The aqueduct served the short-lived Glasgow, Paisley and Johnstone Canal before being converted to a railway viaduct in 1885.

built in the first half of the eighteenth century were for drainage, hydrological control or ornament, or a combination of these purposes (for example the canal at Mavisbank House, Midlothian). Serious preparatory surveys for a Forth-Clyde canal were undertaken in the 1710s and 1720s, but foundered through lack of money. In 1741, when Edinburgh Town Council revived the idea again, Scotland's 'Universal Architect', William Adam, looked to France, the Low Countries and England for examples that might serve as a model for the proposed canal:

I have seen all the most considerable ones [canals] both in Holland & England but those at Ostend & Dunkirk are certainly the noblest and best disposed things I have seen, and I can venture to say I am as much master of the form & Disposition of them as the building of an House.[8]

However, it was the huge success and engineering wonder of the 3rd Duke of Bridgewater's coal canal serving Manchester, designed by the engineer James Brindley and opened in 1761, that finally provided the confidence and the finance to take

forward a major scheme by John Smeaton for the Forth and Clyde Canal in 1764.

The moral philospher and father of modern economics, Adam Smith, recognised in his seminal work, *An Inquiry into the Nature and Causes of the Wealth of Nations*, of 1776 that 'Good roads, canals, and navigable rivers, by diminishing the expence of carriage, put the remote parts of the country more nearly upon a level with those in the neighbourhood of the town. They are upon that account the greatest of all improvements. They encourage the cultivation of the remote, which must always be the most extensive circle of the country. They are advantageous to the town by breaking down the monopoly of the country in its neighbourhood.' Writing in 1830, Sir David Brewster, the eminent physicist, mathematician, astronomer, inventor, historian and writer described the considerable benefits of the new canals over the turnpike road system:

The advantages derived from inland navigation are now so generally known and acknowledged, that the statement of a very few facts seems quite sufficient to show its utility.

1. When bulky articles, or those of great weight, are to be moved with great regularity in a short time, inland navigation is the best mode in which this can be accomplished.

2. Agriculture and manufactures profit equally; and the country at large is, by this means, at all times assured of an equal and ready distribution of food and fuel. By diminishing the number of draught horses also, a greater proportion of the produce of the earth is appropriated to the support of man; and the facility of conveyance affords the means of opening districts which would otherwise remain unimproved.

3. The capital saved in the article of transport is, of course, appropriated to more productive labour. To convey 20 tons upon a narrow canal, the horse and boat generally cost about £100 and require

only one man and a boy. To carry the same weight by land, more than 20 such horses are required, and at least 10 men. The land establishment would therefore cost at least ten times the expense of that by the canal, under a proportionably greater tear and wear.

4. Against this saving is to be put only the original proper extra cost of the canal and its appendages, over that of a turnpike road and its bridges and other works. The results may be distinctly ascertained, by considering that the total expense of carriage upon canals is only about one-third of that by land, besides its enabling much larger quantities to be conveyed over the same space in the same time; so that whenever an industrious population has increased to a certain extent, this mode of conveyance has invariably been resorted to.

5. The intimate connection between inland navigation, and irrigation and draining, has likewise operated powerfully in promoting the former...[9]
These factors were to underpin the craze for canals in Scotland that stemmed from the successful development of the Forth and Clyde Canal.

CANAL MANIA, 1760–1840
The following chapters of this book examine the development of the five surviving major canals in Scotland, but it is worth mentioning here the

other navigational canals that were completed or started, and the plethora that were planned but not implemented.

Of the completed canals, the most substantial contour canal was the eighteen-mile Aberdeenshire Canal from the harbour in Aberdeen to Port Elphinstone in Inverurie, designed by John Rennie and commenced in 1796.[10] It opened in 1805, carrying granite, lime, coal, bark for paper-making, agricultural products and passengers, but was abandoned in 1854 to make way for the Great North of Scotland Railway. Only a short section remains in water at Port Elphinstone, one original masonry bridge survives at Station Road in Aberdeen, and a number of milestones can also be found, although not all in their original locations.

The Glasgow, Paisley and Ardrossan Canal, promoted by the 12th Earl of Eglinton, terminated at Johnstone only seven miles from Port Eglinton in Glasgow in 1811. This contour canal had a complicated genesis involving some of the best engineers and surveyors of the day, including William Jessop, John Rennie, John Ainslie and Thomas Telford.[11] The canal never reached its intended destination of the earl's new harbour at Ardrossan, and suffered a fate similar to the Aberdeenshire Canal in 1881 at the hands of the Glasgow and South Western Railway. Another canal was designed by James Watt in 1768 to connect the Forth and Clyde Canal

Sir W.G. Armstrong Whitworth & Co., View of the Proposed Mid-Scotland Ship Canal as Seen from Stirling, about 1917
Glasgow University Archives Service

Proposals for an enlarged ship canal between the Rivers Forth and Clyde first emerged in the 1880s. The military and strategic benefits of such a scheme were at the forefront of this proposal, drawn up towards the end of the First World War.

Copy of an Act of Parliament Printed in London by Charles Eyre and William Strahan, 1784
Scottish Life Archive

The paper contains the terms and conditions of the Act that extended the powers of an earlier Act to build the Forth and Clyde canal.

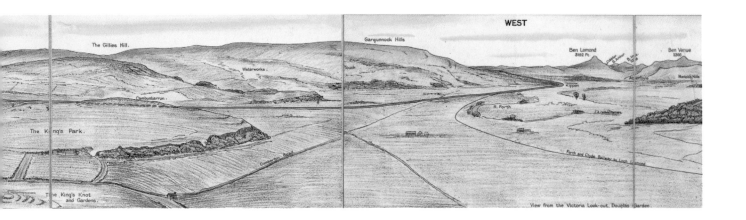

WEST

View from the Victoria Look-out. Douglas Garden

with the port of Bo'ness, but it remained incomplete and was abandoned in 1797.[12]

All the other completed or partly-completed canals were less than three miles in length and built for single users, small groups of private individuals or companies. These included the Burnturk Canal (opened about 1800, limeworks), Campbeltown Canal (1794, coal), Carlingwark Canals (1765 and 1768, shell-marl), Carron Canal (1781, iron works), Dingwall Canal (1819, improved navigation), Fleet Canal (1824, improved navigation), the Forth and Cart Junction Canal (1840, navigational short-cut), Kilbagie Canal (1780, distillery), Muirkirk Canal (about 1789, coal and iron ore), St Fergus and River Ugie Canal (after 1793, shell-sand) and the Stevenston Canal (1772, coal).[13]

The author of the pioneering work on Scotland's canals, Jean Lindsay, has identified dozens of canals that were proposed but never built.[14] Some made it as far as parliamentary approval, while others remained little more than glimmers in their proposers' eyes. Again, significant surveyors and engineers were involved in these abortive projects. For example, James Watt planned a scheme to link the alum works at Hurlet to Paisley and two potential canal routes in Perthshire and Angus in 1770: from the Linn of Campsie to Crieff; and from Perth via Coupar Angus to Forfar.[15] Both

(959)

ANNO VICESIMO QUARTO

Georgii III. Regis.

C A P. LIX.

An Act for extending, amending, and altering the Powers of an Act, made in the Eighth Year of the Reign of His present Majesty, intituled, *An Act for making and maintaining a Navigable Cut or Canal from the Firth or River of* Forth, *at or near the Mouth of the River of* Carron, *in the County of* Stirling, *to the Firth or River of* Clyde, *at or near a Place called* Dalmuir Burnfoot, *in the County of* Dumbarton; *and also a Collateral Cut from the same to the City of* Glasgow; *and for making a Navigable Cut or Canal of Communication from the Port and Harbour of* Borrowstounness, *to join the said Canal at or near the Place where it will fall into the Firth of* Forth.

11 K 2   WHEREAS,

Forth and Clyde Share Certificate, 1851
Glasgow University Archives Service

With the exception of the Caledonian Canal, shareholder companies constructed and ran all the canals. From the outset the University of Glasgow was an active investor in the two Glasgow canals, the Forth and Clyde and the Monkland. The factor to the University, Matthew Morthland, also served as the treasurer for the Monkland Canal Company. These investments were the source of some controversy within the University.

James Hopkirk, The Kelvin Aqueduct carrying the Forth and Clyde Canal across the River Kelvin, 1829 →
Glasgow University Library, Special Collections

When it opened in 1790, the Kelvin Aqueduct was the largest aqueduct in Europe. Designed by Robert Whitworth and built by William Gibb and John Muir of Falkirk, it was considered one of the wonders of the age. Hopkirk's drawing shows a two-masted vessel on its way to the canal's terminus at Bowling on the River Clyde. Gibb, the founder of the famous engineering dynasty, made a huge loss on the contract rather than missing the construction deadline.

Robert Stevenson (1812) and John Rennie (before 1818) re-surveyed Robert Whitworth's proposed route (1788) for an extension of the Strathmore Canal between Forfar and Arbroath.[16] Stevenson surveyed another route from Perth to Loch Earn, which became the basis of a parliamentary bill for the Tay Canal in 1807.[17]

While the active trading days of the old canals were numbered by 1888, an interest in a new large-scale Mid-Scotland Ship Canal began to ferment. This revival of attention on water transport was due in large part to the start of work on the enormous Manchester Ship Canal in 1887 and the consequent excitement in other major industrial cities around the British Isles. The Mid-Scotland Canal project was to provoke rivalries between Glasgow, Edinburgh and Leith that echoed the discussions over earlier canal projects. The Edinburgh engineers, D. & T. Stevenson, presented an options study in 1889 favouring a Loch Lomond route for a thirty-foot deep and eighty-foot wide Mid-Scotland Canal, which would meet both military and mercantile needs.[18] Almost immediately a rival Glasgow committee commissioned the Glasgow engineers, Crouch & Hogg, to consider a more direct route to the city from the River Forth. Arguments over the route, dimensions, design and costs of the proposed canal continued intermittently well into the twentieth century, concluding with Sir John Graham Kerr's grand scheme of 1942.[19]

PLANNING AND FINANCE

The building of canals required a considerable amount of planning and preparation by various parties, including promoters, surveyors, engineers, landowners, lawyers, politicians and investors. In most cases the promoters of canals were those with a financial interest in improving transport links to their lands or businesses. Informal groups of promoters came together around particular schemes, and then using their own resources commissioned a survey of the potential routes and initial estimates of construction costs and operational revenues. In some instances, such as

the Forth and Clyde and Union Canals, rival groups of promoters supported different routes to achieve similar aims. Level, or contour, canals were generally preferred, even if they took longer routes, as they avoided the expensive construction of locks and the delays of locks in operation.

With the establishment of a widely acceptable route and budget, the next stage in the development of a canal project was to gather subscriptions, or promises of money, towards the construction costs. This was normally done by means of agents, newspaper advertising and a prospectus, which set out the benefits of the scheme, the route, the dimensions, the costs and the proposed dues and anticipated revenues. Without exception, the prospectuses underestimated construction and maintenance costs, and overestimated the revenues. The 1792 prospectus for the Crinan Canal, for example, estimated an annual total of lockage dues at £2,254 and eleven shillings, based on a proposed due of one shilling per ton.[20] In fact the total revenues only reached that level in 1841, by which time the annual standard operational expenditure was

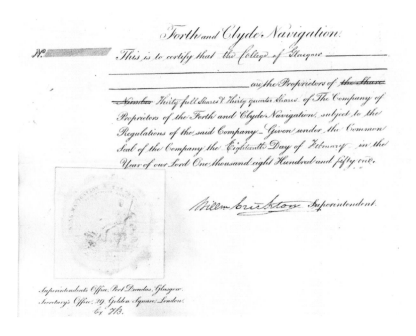

The Sea Lock at Clachnaharry on the Caledonian Canal copied from *Atlas to the Life of Thomas Telford* (London, 1838) and engraved by Edmund Turrell ↓
RCAHMS

The sea lock at Clachnaharry, designed by Thomas Telford, is one of the great engineering achievements of the canal age in Scotland. In order to counter-reach a reasonable depth of water in the Beauly Firth, two 400-foot-long artificial mounds were constructed to continue the Caledonian Canal out into the firth. Telford developed a new method of pre-consolidating the subsoil to counter the difficult ground conditions for constructing the sea lock here.

£1,573.[21] Other canals, such as the Aberdeenshire and Union Canals, operated tonnage-per-mile duties, for which stone mileposts were erected to aid the fee calculations.

Having gathered sufficient promises of funding to cover the construction costs, the promoters needed to seek parliamentary approval by means of a private bill. Committees of both Houses of Parliament scrutinised the proposals. The committees were subject to lobbying by influential landowners, businesses and even town councils, and numerous canal schemes failed at this stage. If the proposers were successful in parliament, the authorising Act usually set out a route, a financial limit for the project, the level of dues, and also enabled the formation of a commercial canal company to manage the construction project and subsequent operation of the canal.

The companies then set about share issues to raise the promised capital, appointed a chief engineer to take forward the detailed design and construction, and began negotiations with landowners to purchase the necessary land and construction access rights. These last actions were frequently fraught with difficulties: many subscribers failed to pay for their shares; detailed survey work on the route revealed poor ground conditions requiring expensive mitigation; and some landowners proved unreasonable, demanding expensive deviations in the route or seeking unrealistic sums above the market rate for the land. A number of canal companies took out loans to cover the difference between the promised amounts and

Lock-keepers' Cottages at Bowling on the Forth and Clyde Canal
RCAHMS

These lock-keepers' cottages were designed by the distinguished Glasgow architectural practice of John Burnet, Son and Campbell and were built in 1896. They are the only Arts and Crafts lock-keepers' houses on the canal and were built for the then owners of the canal, the Caledonian Railway Company. They also form part of an important group of structures at the western entrance to the canal which includes the locks and the former customs house.

the receipts from investors, adding interest costs to the schemes. The capital costs of all the surviving canals came in at more than twice the level estimated by their promoters.[22] Time and again funding and construction difficulties forced canal companies to return to Parliament for new legislation to vary the route or the financial limits.[23]

CONSTRUCTION

Having cleared the preparatory hurdles, the real work of building the canal began. It was necessary for the canal companies to assemble a small army of construction workers including resident engineers, surveyors, overseers, foremen, specialist and general contractors and 'navigators' or 'navvies'. The chief engineers were responsible for controlling financial matters relating to the construction and reporting directly to the canal companies, or in the case of the Caledonian Canal, to the commissioners. The scale, complexity and remoteness of the Caledonian Canal, and its part-purpose as a government employment project, made it an exception in many aspects of its planning and construction: here Thomas Telford gathered 'those persons of experience in the several departments of canal labour whom we have found it expedient to encourage to settle on the line of the Caledonian Canal, in order that they may undertake the contracts for work, and by their example impart skill and activity to the persons employed under their direction'.[24]

Resident engineers undertook the day-to-day management of the construction. In many instances this was a lonely and difficult job, keeping on top of a myriad of technical and budgetary issues, demanding employers, obstructive landowners, variable qualities of contractors and the sheer daily grind of enormous and complicated construction projects, frequently in remote locations and inclement conditions.

Beneath the resident engineer, overseers managed the contractors, who assembled their own teams of masons, wrights (carpenters), smiths (ironworkers) and navvies. The contractors'

recruitment and retention of reliable navvies was in many cases a problem, particularly where the labourers were drawn from local agricultural or fishing communities, where the seasonal requirements of harvesting, planting, herring fishing and peat-cutting took precedence. Similarly, good masons, wrights and smiths were drawn away if higher-paying jobs in more clement locations became available. A number of the navvies on the various canal projects were hard-living and hard-drinking itinerant labourers from the Highlands, Ireland and England, and regularly feuds developed between the navvies themselves or difficulties arose with the local communities. The two principal methods of paying workers were day-rates and piecemeal for each completed unit of work.

Teams of contractors tendered for the various aspects of the construction by individual trade including: excavation and puddling (waterproofing with a malleable paste of puddle clay and fine sand or gravel); fabrication of locks and basins; building of bridges and aqueducts; construction of reservoirs and dams; and digging of drainage and supply channels. The canal companies issued their own tenders for materials such as timber and iron and took leases on local quarries for stone.

Apart from the building of the canal itself, cottages were required for the lock-keepers and bridge-keepers, houses for the canal company officials, stables for the horses, and shipbuilding yards

Maryhill Locks
Nick Haynes

The impressive sequence of five locks and basins at Maryhill was designed by Robert Whitworth and constructed between 1787 and 1790 to lower the canal forty feet from its summit level before crossing the River Kelvin via the spectacular Kelvin Aqueduct.

and graving docks for fabricating and repairing the boats. A whole host of other structures including warehouses, industrial works, factories, inns and workers' housing also grew up around the basins and terminals of the canals.

The chief engineer marked out the route of the canal with wooden stakes, typically at a distance of 150 feet apart, using a theodolite to establish the level and chains to measure the distances. The resident engineer would then supervise the digging of holes to mark the correct depth and width of the canal. Using picks, hand-shovels and wheelbarrows, navvies completed the excavation by connecting the holes with trenches and removing the spoil to form the banks and towpaths. The channel was waterproofed with puddle clay, packed by 'clicking', or treading with specially designed boots, to a depth of up to three feet along the base and one foot along the sides. Puddling was expensive, so it was minimised or avoided where ground conditions allowed. Digging took place in the summer months, while lining was typically a winter job (when the puddle clay could be kept moist more easily). During the refurbishment of the Caledonian Canal in the 1840s, the opportunity was taken to line the tops of the channel sides with large stones to protect them from the damaging wash of steam vessels.

Perhaps the most characteristic and endlessly fascinating features of the canals are the locks to

raise and lower boats between different levels of water. The very first 'land-lock' in Scotland was the temporary structure designed by John Smeaton to carry construction materials for the Forth and Clyde Canal via the River Carron. It was the cause of considerable excitement and curiosity in 1769.[25] Still today the passage of a boat through a lock or flight of locks is frequently accompanied by a crowd of spectators. Often the construction of the locks presented significant challenges of engineering and soil mechanics, and once completed they required high levels of maintenance and repair. Huge pits were dug and kept clear of water, then masons lined the base and sides with layers of rubble and finally dressed sandstone set in hydraulic lime mortar. The early canal lock-gates were made of great oak timbers with wrought-iron framing. Later gates were constructed of cast iron, as Robert Stevenson noted in 1817: 'Lock-gates of cast iron have been for a considerable time in use. Perhaps the first of these were constructed on Carron River, upon a small dock for the repair of the Carron Company's ships'.[26] Only in the second half of the twentieth century did mechanisation ease the task of opening the lock-gates.

Of all the locks, the sea locks, regulating the entrances to the ship canals were the most diffi-cult to build and maintain. At the extraordinary Clachnaharry sea lock on the Caledonian Canal, two artificial 400-foot-long mounds of boulder clay and quarry waste with vertical cores of imper-vious puddle clay were constructed out into the Beauly Firth to create the canal between them. The settlement of the mounds required the addition of another layer of waste material eleven feet in depth. Subsidence was a considerable problem in the construction of all the locks, where a substan-tial weight of masonry was added to the natural ground conditions. As a result of the settlement issues of the canal walls at Clachnaharry, Telford developed 'a new method, one at least which I had not known to have been elsewhere practiced', which involved creating a mound of waste materials and loose stones at the site in order to compress, or

The Avon Aqueduct, Union Canal

RCAHMS

The Avon Aqueduct carries the Union Canal across the valley of the River Avon and its wooded valley to the south-west of Linlithgow. Built between 1818 and 1822, to a design by Hugh Baird, it is the longest and tallest aqueduct in Scotland.

Laughing and Greeting Faces on Bridge Sixty-one on the Union Canal
Nick Haynes

The two faces of this bridge, which was built in 1821, look in opposite directions: the laughing face towards the east and the greeting (crying) face to the west. It is thought that the faces symbolise the contractors, who made money on the works to the east, but lost money on the tunnel to the west.

Linlithgow Bridge, Union Canal
Peter Sandground

Apart from a flight of locks at the Falkirk end, the Union Canal is all on the same level. It was built with fixed bridges to take barges. This view shows the bridge at the canal basin.

'pre-consolidate', the subsoil of the pit for a year before the construction of the masonry.[27] The Falkirk Wheel, the world's only rotating canal boatlift, has brought lock technology into the twenty-first century.

The Forth and Clyde Canal was pioneering not only in its use of locks, but also in the construction of Scotland's first significant aqueduct, the Luggie Aqueduct, in Kirkintilloch, designed by John Smeaton, and then the world's longest navigable aqueduct over the River Kelvin. Robert Whitworth's 445-foot long Kelvin Aqueduct became the wonder of the age on its opening in 1790, with crowds gathering along the banks of the River Kelvin to witness the 'singular and new object of a vessel navigation 70 feet over their heads …'[28] Although widened and converted to a railway bridge (and now to a cycle path), the Blackhall Aqueduct over the White Cart Water in Paisley is Scotland's largest single span canal aqueduct (eighty-eight feet, six inches), designed

Banavie Railway Swing Bridge, Caledonian Canal
Nick Haynes

Opened in 1901, the swing bridge carries the Fort William to Mallaig railway line over the Caledonian Canal at the foot of Banavie Locks (Neptune's Staircase).

Swing Bridge at Muirtown Basin, Caledonian Canal
Nick Haynes

The Muirtown Swing Bridge carries the A862 over the Caledonian Canal. Built in 1935 by Sir William Arrol & Co., it replaced an earlier bridge.

and built between 1808 and 1810 under the supervision of Thomas Telford for the Glasgow, Paisley and Johnstone Canal.[29] Most canals employed aqueducts of varying scales to cross roads and rivers, but by far the largest and most spectacular aqueducts were those designed by Hugh Baird with advice from Thomas Telford for the Union Canal over the Water of Leith, River Almond and River Avon. Unlike the all-masonry Kelvin Aqueduct, the Union Canal aqueducts carry the water in a cast-iron trough, which enables them to be narrower, taller and require less masonry.

Bridges were, and remain, numerous on all the canals and vary in type according to the nature of the canal: bascule (lifting) and swing bridges for the ship canals; and fixed masonry bridges for the other canals. Many of the fixed bridges survive in place over the Union Canal. However, none of the original moveable bridges remain without replacement or alteration. The wear on the moving parts, changing user demands, or the deficiencies in design (for example the need for two operators of a manual double bascule bridge) led to constant refinements and replacements. Robert Stevenson described the differences between the old bridges on the Forth and Clyde Canal and the new ones on the Caledonian Canal in 1817:

Canal Bridges were formerly constructed of timber, and lifted in two leaves or halves by chains and a large timber framing; but they are now chiefly framed of cast iron, the roadway only being covered with timber; and by the latest improvements they are raised by a wheel and pinion, as originally projected by Mr Perronnet [Jean-Rodolphe Perronet (1708–94), engineer to the king of France, Louis XV] for the Neva, at St Petersburgh, and now introduced on the Forth and Clyde Canal, or as here managed, they are made to turn in two pieces, each placed upon an opposite abutment of masonry, and move upon a centre, similar to those of the West India and London Docks. The compartments which project over the water way of the canal, meet and joggle

Twechar Bridge, Forth and Clyde Canal
RCAHMS

This lifting bridge was constructed in 1960 by Sir William Arrol & Co., shortly before the closure of the canal. The abutments of the original bascule bridge remained intact alongside the new structure.

The landowner of Callendar Park,
Sir William Forbes, was one of the
major obstacles to the construction
of the Union Canal. He commissioned
the renowned artist and engineer
Alexander Nasmyth to produce
images showing how damaging the
canal would be to his estate. This
view of 'part of the track of the injurious
deviation from the Parliamentary Line
of the Edinburgh and Glasgow Union
Canal', shows a parade of canal boats
and horses overlooking Callendar
Park. Forbes' objections were
eventually overcome by the expensive construction of the Prospect
Hill Tunnel.

into each other, while the opposite ends, towards
the land, are loaded so as to become a counterpoise
to the projecting parts.[30]

New bridges were added to the canals, or existing
bridges modified, to meet the requirements of the
expanding railway and road networks. The railway
companies used swing bridges over the canals on
the Highland Line at Clachnaharry (1862; rebuilt
in 1909), on the West Highland Line at Banavie
(1901), on the Caledonian Railway's Port Dundas
branch (about 1890), and on the Lanarkshire and
Dunbartonshire Railway at Bowling. Amongst
numerous fixed railway bridges were the major
structures of 1870–2 and 1898 over the Monkland
Canal, which still dominate the heart of Coatbridge,
although the canal itself is now culverted at
this location. With the rapid expansion of motor
transport in the 1920s and 1930s, the Ministry of
Transport began a major programme of upgrading
and enlarging the road swing bridges along the
Caledonian Canal, employing the eminent engineering firm of Sir William Arrol & Co., which had
been responsible for the construction of the Forth
Bridge and Tower Bridge in London. New road
bridges were required over the Forth and Clyde and
Union Canals as part of the Millennium Link project
in 1998–2002. In a reversal of previous trends,
the very latest fixed and lifting bridges have been
constructed at the M9 and the A905 near Helix
Park in Falkirk to enable the extension of the Forth
and Clyde Canal to the new River Carron sea lock.

Cuttings through slopes were relatively common
to all the canals, but tunnels were expensive

and therefore rare. Two existed on the Glasgow,
Paisley and Johnstone Canal, one on a branch of
the Monkland Canal, and by far the longest was
built on the Union Canal to avoid disruption to the
landowner's gaze at Callendar Park, Falkirk. Later
railway tunnels under the canals, for example at
Stobcross and Knightswood on the Forth and Clyde
Canal, effectively created new aqueducts carrying
the canals over the railways. Little-recognised
elements of the canal network are the numerous
reservoirs and feeder channels, culverts and sluices
built to control and maintain year-round water levels
and to feed the water-hungry locks.

OPERATION AND MAINTENANCE

The prospectuses for the canals had little to say
about the anticipated operational and maintenance
costs. The capital costs of construction were so
great that there was significant pressure to start
generating income, in a number of cases before the
canal was properly complete. The rush to finish the
Crinan Canal and the Caledonian Canal resulted
in shoddy workmanship in places, which was to
cause problems later. Inevitably, such large pieces
of infrastructure involving water management
needed a high level of staffing, equipment and
maintenance to ensure safe operation. Staffing
varied from company to company, but could include
a permanent resident engineer, a collector of dues,
superintendents, pilots, masons, blacksmiths,
banksmen and general labourers. Each group of
locks and every major bascule or swing bridge
required at least one canal company keeper (usually
a carpenter) and their accompanying housing.

Carron Company Lighter Number Six Passing the Old Granary on the Forth and Clyde Canal at Bankside, Bainsford, about 1890
Falkirk Archives

Boatmen's Institute, Port Dundas, Glasgow
Glasgow Museums and Libraries Collection

The institute was founded to give canal bargemen a place to spend their leisure hours other than the public house. The organisation dated from 1870, but new premises were built in about 1890, to designs by Honeyman & Keppie. The design of the steeple is based on that of the seventeenth-century Old College of Glasgow, then recently demolished. After the decline of boat traffic on the canal in the 1940s the Boatmen's Institute became effectively a community centre for the residents of the Port Dundas area. It was demolished about 1966 to make way for an urban motorway. The firm's draughtsman, Charles Rennie Mackintosh, is believed to have contributed to the designs.

Forth and Clyde Canal, Falkirk

Bargemen's Institute
Port Dundas
Honeyman and Keppie

Periodic dredging was needed, and in winter special ice-breaking barges were used to keep the waterways clear.

The Forth and Clyde Canal Company initially ran two of its own 'track-boats for transporting goods and passengers', but from 1809 the passengers were provided with separate boats for their increased comfort.[31] Horsepower was the only means of propulsion along the canals of the late eighteenth century. However, increasingly efficient steam engines prompted a number of early experiments with steam propulsion:

After Mr Patrick Miller and Mr Symington had, on Dalswinton Loch, proved the feasibility of using steam on the water, they came to Edinburgh, and had a boat of 30 tons burthen constructed at Carron. In November 1789 this vessel was launched on the Forth and Clyde Canal. In presence of hundreds of people the vessel started, and attained a speed of 6 miles an hour. On reaching Lock 16 unhappily the floats of the paddlewheels gave way,
and the experiment had to be stopped. Ten years later Lord Dundas desired Symington to construct a steamer to be used as a tug on the canal, and in March 1802 the Charlotte Dundas towed two laden barges of 70 tons burthen each a distance of 19½ miles with great ease.[32]

Another pioneering experiment on the Forth and Clyde Canal was the operation of 'Vulcan', the world's first iron-hulled vessel, designed by Henry Creighton in 1819 to carry 200 passengers and their luggage. The use of horses on the Lowland canals to draw the flat-bottomed 'scows' or 'lighters' (bulk-carrying barges) continued long after the advent of steam power and the introduction of Puffers. By contrast, steam power was transforming the nature of water-borne transport as the Highland canals were under construction. Here, steam tugs and Puffers predominated in the second half of the nineteenth century, and one, the 'Auld Reekie', continued in use into the 1970s. The Puffers plied their trade on the canals and also around the West

Schooner Accident on the Caledonian Canal, 1881
Inverness Museum and Art Gallery

Accidents on the canals were frequent, but images recording them are rare. In this photograph two schooners block the Caledonian Canal at Clachnaharry, Inverness. The 'Regent', which was registered in Inverness, was bound for Cardiff while the 'Progress', from the Isle of Man was carrying coal to Muirtown.

Coast and Hebridean islands. Neil Munro's Para Handy stories of the early 1900s for the *Glasgow Evening News* were based around the fictional Puffer, 'Vital Spark'. Diesel engines began to replace steam power in the early twentieth century.

From the outset, accidents and drownings were common occurrences on the canals. Swimming and life-saving were not generally taught as they are now. The dereliction of the urban canals in the twentieth century made them increasingly dangerous. Crashes between boats or with lock-gates or the banks were also frequent. These became more serious in the steam age, when speeds were greater and slowing down took longer. Precautionary measures were introduced, including the lining of cast-iron gates with timber to soften the impact, and the provision of protective chains across the approaches to the locks on the Caledonian Canal.

The twenty-first-century renaissance of the waterways has seen a diverse range of activities on and around the canals, from leisure cruising, fishing, paddling, canoeing and rowing to walking, jogging, cycling, photography and art workshops, archaeology and special events, together with a wide range of catering and retail outlets. Now operation of the canals involves not just the management of the structural integrity and safety of the waterways, but also the promotion of community life, tourism, economic development, ecology, environment, culture, heritage, health, education, regeneration and sustainable development.

Forth and Clyde Canal

Customs House, Bowling
Nick Haynes

Bowling is the western terminus of the Forth and Clyde Canal. The Customs House was built around 1800. The iron swing bridge to the east of the Customs House was built in 1896 to designs by Crouch & Hogg for the Lanarkshire & Dunbartonshire Railway.

Nor can I refrain mentioning how easy a Work it would be to form a Navigation, I mean a Navigation of Art from the Forth to the Clyde, and so join the two Seas, as the King of France has done in a place five times as far, and five Hundred times as difficult, namely from Thoulouze to Narbonne. What an Advantage in Commerce would this be, opening the Irish Trade to the Merchants of Glasgow, making a Communication between the West Coast of Scotland, and the East Coast of England, and even to London itself; nay, several Ports of England, on the Irish Sea, from Liverpool Northward, would all Trade with London by such a Canal, it would take up a Volume by itself, to lay down the several Advantages to the Trade of Scotland, that would immediately occur by such a Navigation, and then to give a true Survey of the Ground, the Easiness of its being perform'd, and the probable Charge of it, all which might be done: But it is too much to undertake here, it must lye till posterity, by the rising Greatness of their Commerce, shall not only feel the Want of it, but find themselves able for the Performance.

Daniel Defoe, *A tour thro' the whole island of Great Britain, Divided into Circuits or Journies*, 1724.[1]

At thirty-five miles in length, from Grangemouth in the east to Bowling in the west, and costing some £330,000, the 'Great Canal' represented the largest private capital project of eighteenth-century Scotland.[2] The canal was similarly ambitious and pioneering in its engineering achievement, involving the construction of Scotland's first land-lock, its first large-scale aqueduct and the largest manmade reservoir of the time. It took some twenty-two years to construct the thirty-five miles of the main canal, and a further year to complete the nearly three mile subsidiary canal to Port Dundas in Glasgow and the one mile link to the Monkland Canal. On opening in July 1790, the canal comprised: a channel eight feet deep, fifty-six feet wide at the surface and twenty-eight feet wide at the bottom; a towpath; twenty locks to raise the canal to the summit of

A Description of Part of the Highlands of Scotland copied by John Manson, about 1748
National Library of Scotland, Edinburgh

This is a detail from a map marking the clan territories in Scotland from the Lothians, Ayrshire and Renfrewshire in the south to Kintail in the north. The map shows the Antonine Wall, named as 'Graham's Dike', the Roman fort at Ardoch, and an early proposed route for the Forth and Clyde Canal. This route probably relates to the survey undertaken by Alexander Gordon in 1726.

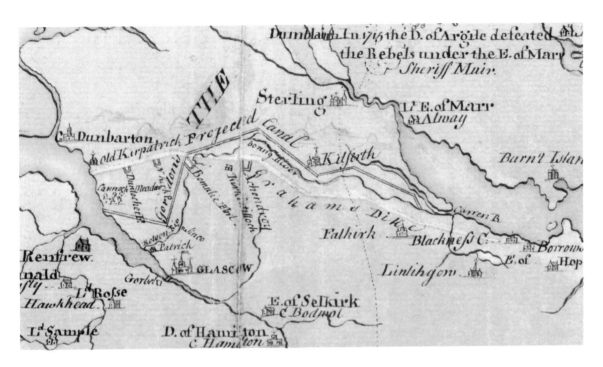

its route 156 feet above the low water of the River Forth, and another nineteen locks to lower it back to the level of the River Clyde; six reservoirs covering 409 acres and supplying 12,679 lockfuls of water; thirty-three bascule bridges and drawbridges; ten large aqueducts and thirty-three smaller ones; a dry dock; and a number of basins for loading of goods.[3] The journey from firth to firth by horse-drawn barge could be made in less than eighteen hours.

PLANNING THE CANAL, SEVENTEENTH AND EIGHTEENTH CENTURIES

The military and trading advantages of a link between the Irish Sea and the North Sea were recognised from the first suggestion of a Forth-Clyde ship canal in the second half of the seventeenth century.[4] Both warships and trading vessels would be able to avoid the long and dangerous passage around the north coasts of Scotland and through the Pentland Firth. The main trade benefits were identified as opening up the West of Scotland

to trade with the Baltic countries and enabling the East of Scotland direct access to the Atlantic trading routes. In time of war with France or Spain, the Baltic states could continue to trade safely with the West Indies and Americas, using the canal rather than the English Channel or northern routes. The canal could also carry bulky loads that were simply not possible overland via rough roads with horse-drawn carts.

The surveyor John Adair carried out the first serious attempt to plot canal routes between the two rivers in the early years of the eighteenth century.[5] One potential route started on the River Forth above Stirling, passed through Loch Lomond and then on to the River Clyde. The other route considered was the one that was adopted in large part when the scheme came to be built in the 1760s: from the River Carron through the central lowlands to a point six miles downstream of Glasgow on the River Clyde. Adair appears to have revisited the canal proposals sometime after 1710 in the company of the architects James Smith and Alexander

Plan of that Part of the Great Canal with Temporary Cut, Timber Basin which Occupies Part of the Lands of Kerse by Hugh Baird
Scottish Canals

This plan of 1817 by Hugh Baird shows the planned layout of Grangemouth, the eastern terminus of the Forth and Clyde Canal. Sir Lawrence Dundas, the governor of the canal company, began construction of a new village at Grangemouth on his own lands of Kerse in 1777, much to the annoyance of nearby Bo'ness, which was long-established as a port. By the 1790s Grangemouth was handling timber, flax and iron from the Baltic, Norway and Sweden, grain from other continental markets, 9,360 tons of goods from the Carron Shipping Company and coal from Scotland and England.

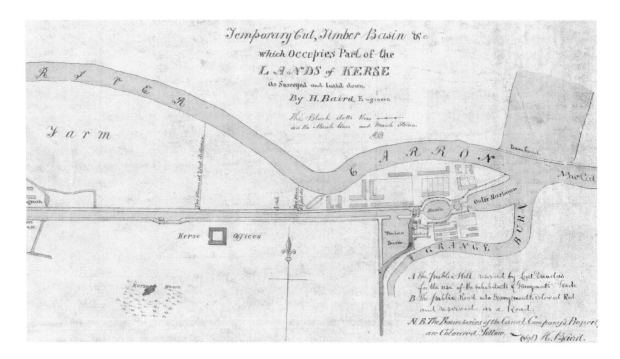

McGill and the eminent Derbyshire engineer George Sorocold.[6] Alexander Gordon, an antiquary and musician, made a further survey of a potential canal route in 1726.[7] The architect William Adam, who had made a particular study of the canal engineering at Bruges and Dunkirk, examined Gordon's proposal and took great interest in Edinburgh Town Council's plan to revive the scheme in 1741.[8] William Pitt the Elder's state-funded proposal of 1760 collapsed on his resignation in the following year. However, there was increasing commercial interest in the project, culminating in surveys by Robert Mackell and James Murray for Lord Napier in 1762 and finally by John Smeaton for the Board of Trustees for the Encouragement of Fisheries, Manufactures and Improvements in Scotland in 1764. Smeaton's first report, which like Adair's proposal presented two options, was hotly contested by various competing interest groups, including the tobacco merchants of Glasgow, the Carron Iron Company, and the merchants of Bo'ness and Edinburgh.[9] Smeaton's second scheme, which adopted the central

lowland route and bypassed Glasgow, was also much debated.[10] After significant wrangling and amendment relating to the route and dimensions of the canal, the Act for making and maintaining a navigable Canal from the Firth or River of Forth, at or near the mouth of the River Carron, in the county of Stirling, to the Firth or River of Clyde, at or near a place called Dalmuir Burnfoot, in the county of Dumbarton; and also a collateral Cut from the same to the city of Glasgow; and for making a navigable Cut or Canal of Communication from the Port or Harbour of Borrowstounness, to join the said Canal at or near the place where it will fall into the Firth of Forth received Royal Assent on 8 March 1768.[11] The preamble to the Act stated the purpose of the canal to be: the promotion of trade between the two firths; the improvement of adjacent lands; the relief of the poor; the preservation of the public roads; and general utility. The Company of Proprietors of the Forth and Clyde Navigation funded the estimated £150,000 project through the issue of 1,500 shares at £100 each.[12] The Lords Provost of Edinburgh and Glasgow held shares in the interests of their respective cities, along with the Lord Privy Seal of Scotland, the Lord Advocate and numerous aristocrats, landed gentry and merchants.

BUILDING THE CANAL, 1768–90

The company appointed John Smeaton as engineer-in-chief and Robert Mackell as his deputy. Smeaton initially envisaged three sections of canal being constructed simultaneously at the east, west and centre of the route, but in the end the work was planned to progress systematically from east to west.[13] In order to manage the huge project, Smeaton set out a 'Plan or Model for carrying on the mechanical Part of the Works of the Canal from Forth to Clyde', in which he presided over the resident engineer (Mackell), a surveyor and the foremen of digging, carpentry and masonry. The resident engineer was to mark out the grounds for purchase, draw up detailed plans for each section of canal, and to survey and purchase the materials, liaising with the engineer in chief and the committee of the canal company. The surveyor was responsible for the quantities, quality and preparation of the materials, and for orders to the foremen. 'Overmen' led the various gangs of workmen beneath the foremen.

The businessman, politician, landowner, major investor and governor of the canal company, Sir Lawrence Dundas of Kerse, cut the first turf at the Carron Basin on 10 June 1768.[14] Much of the following year was spent gathering equipment, skilled tradesmen (carpenters, smiths, masons) and materials, and in constructing temporary roads and a small lock near Dalgrain.[15] Once the equipment and tradesmen were in place, a small army of navvies was recruited. This varied in number from about 600 to over 1,200 in the course of the project, with harvests drawing men away to their normal work on the land. Work began on the first permanent lock in August 1769, after which progress was rapid. Nine miles of canal were cut and seven locks commenced or completed by the beginning of 1770.[16] Parliament passed the first of a number of amending Acts in March 1771, authorising Robert

Mackell's cost-saving adjustment of the route further south to take the main canal within two miles of Glasgow, and to reduce the length of the Glasgow branch canal.

From 1771 to 1775 the construction of the canal inched westwards through the most challenging ground of Craigmarloch (tough boulder clay, gravel, rocks and hard whinstone) and Dullatur (deep bog) to Stockingfield, where the branch to Glasgow was to fork off. Smeaton's intial cost estimates had not taken account of the difficult geological conditions, and economic conditions worsened during construction. In order to start generating toll income as soon as possible, newly completed sections of the canal were filled with water, and temporary warehouses and carting facilities were provided to connect with Glasgow.[17] Smeaton resigned from the project in 1773, in large part to save the canal company his salary in the straitened times following the 1772 collapse of the Ayr Bank. Robert Mackell served as the effective supervising engineer until his death in 1779. However, by July 1775 the project was in serious financial trouble and work on the main route to Bowling was suspended for nine years. This crisis was caused by a combination of factors including late subscription payments, soaring land and labour prices, and increasing maintenance costs.[18] Funded by the city's merchants, construction continued intermittently on the branch to Glasgow, as this was a key element in making the scheme profitable. It was not until August 1784 that construction resumed at full strength after the government authorised a loan of £50,000 from the proceeds of the landed estates forfeited after the 1745 Jacobite Rising. The canal company appointed Robert Whitworth as their chief engineer in 1785. Whitworth had worked under James Brindley, a pioneering canal engineer in England.

Even at this late stage in the project, design and engineering issues presented significant challenges. Whitworth re-planned the route to the River Clyde to connect at Bowling, about ten miles west of the centre of Glasgow. He also submitted

George Romney (after Rhodes), Portrait of John Smeaton, about 1779
National Portrait Gallery, London

The earliest of four canals built in the Lowlands of Scotland was the Forth and Clyde Canal, which opened from sea to sea on 28 July 1790. It was designed by the extraordinarily prolific John Smeaton (1724–1792) who was one of the first people to call himself a civil engineer. He laid the foundations for the profession of civil engineering, as well as establishing consulting engineering and defining the role of resident engineer. His career mirrored the developments of the Industrial Revolution in Britain. Smeaton's achievements and interests were wide-ranging – from scientific instruments to steam engines, canals to harbours, bridges to lighthouses and mills to astronomy. His most famous work is perhaps Eddystone Lighthouse but he had notable successes with other major civil engineering projects such as Ramsgate Harbour and Perth Bridge.

Section and Plan of a Turning Bridge by John Smeaton, 1768
Royal Society, London

Design for a turning (swing) bridge for the Forth and Clyde Canal. Section and plan, 1:48 scale, from Smeaton volume 5, fol.8. The Forth and Clyde Canal was Smeaton's largest project. The canal provided a route for sea-going vessels by linking the Firth of Forth in the east with the Firth of Clyde in the west. In order to accommodate the masts of sailing ships, the bridges on the canal needed to open to remove any overhead obstruction.

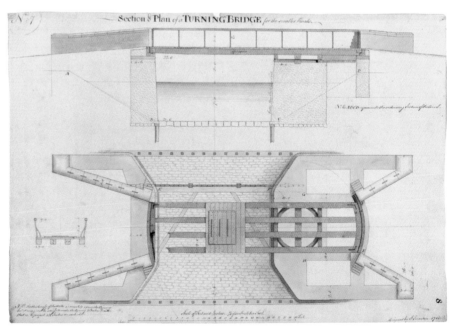

Kennard & Sons, Iron Works, Falkirk, Scotland, about 1855

Science Museum/Science & Society Picture Library

Lithograph by M. Billing showing an aerial view of the huge canalside iron works of Kennard & Sons, which manufactured metal objects including castings for ranges, stove grates, sugar pans, railway chains and girders.

Design by Robert Adam for a Memorial to Mark the Linking of the Rivers Forth and Clyde

Sir John Soane's Museum, London

Scotland's premier architect, Robert Adam, sketched a design for this memorial in 1776. The memorial was never built, and even its intended location is unknown.

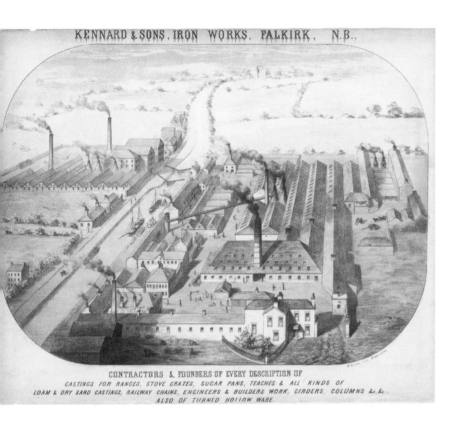

KENNARD & SONS, IRON WORKS, FALKIRK, N.B.

CONTRACTORS & FOUNDERS OF EVERY DESCRIPTION OF
CASTINGS FOR RANGES, STOVE GRATES, SUGAR PANS, TEACHES & ALL KINDS OF
LOAM & DRY SAND CASTINGS, RAILWAY CHAINS, ENGINEERS & BUILDERS WORK, GIRDERS, COLUMNS &c. &c.
ALSO OF TURNED HOLLOW WARE.

a plan to increase the depth of the water along the length of the canal, and proposed a link to the new Monkland Canal. The great wonder of the canal was Whitworth's aqueduct over the River Kelvin and the associated cluster of locks and basins at Maryhill.[19] At the time of its construction by William Gibb and John Moir of Falkirk in 1787–9, the Kelvin Aqueduct was 'supposed the largest fabric of the kind in the world'.[20] Archibald Speirs of Elderslie, governor of the canal company, opened the Great Canal from sea to sea by the ceremonial release of a hogshead of water from the River Forth into the River Clyde at Bowling on 28 July 1790.[21] Work continued on the ports and their infrastructure.

SUCCESSFUL OPERATION, 1790–1842

The revenues of the newly opened canal almost tripled during the course of the 1790s, but it was not until 1800 that dividends were paid to investors and the issue of further stock allowed the repayment of the government loan.[22] In spite of the widespread adverse effects of the Napoleonic Wars on manpower and trade, the canal operated relatively successfully during the first quarter of the nineteenth century. The main direct sources of income to the canal company were from the transport of corn, timber, sugar, herrings and passengers.[23] The introduction in 1809 of comfortable 'swift' or 'fly' passenger boats, towed at a gallop by two thoroughbred horses, saw the construction of substantial stone stables at two mile intervals along the whole canal so that the horses could be changed over and rested. At its heyday in the 1830s, when connected to both the Monkland and Union Canals, the Forth and Clyde carried approximately 200,000 passengers and 460,000 tons of goods annually

James Hopkirk, Two Views of Port Dundas, 1827
Glasgow University Library, Special Collections

Port Dundas was built in the 1780s as the hilltop terminus of the Glasgow Branch of the Forth and Clyde Canal. James Hopkirk's portrayal shows the masts of the boats in the canal basin clustered high above the city and the surrounding countryside. Much of Glasgow's grain was brought into the city along the Forth and Clyde Canal to Port Dundas. Several large granaries were built at the canal terminus to store the grain.

and brought in revenue of between £40,000 and £50,000.[24] As anticipated, the opening of the canal stimulated the development of new communities and businesses around the route, including mines and quarries, shipbuilding yards, iron foundries, smelters, chemical works, engineering workshops, distilleries, breweries, glassworks, timberyards and grain warehouses. Grangemouth, Kirkintilloch, Port Dundas and Bowling all flourished as canal communities and ports.

DECLINE AND CLOSURE, 1842–1963

The threat to the success of the canal emerged in the form of the Edinburgh and Glasgow Railway, which was constructed on an almost parallel route between 1838 and 1842. Passenger traffic dropped away from the canal immediately, and a series of tariff wars with the railway made serious dents in the goods traffic and revenue. The canal company attempted a number of successful initiatives to counter the railway threat, including the introduction of steam power and screw-propellers to their goods 'lighters' or barges and the improvement of access and harbour facilities at Grangemouth. By 1867, when the Caledonian Railway Company purchased the Forth and Clyde Navigation (which by then also included the Monkland Canal), the annual goods carried stood at about three million tons and revenue was approximately £87,000.[25] The Caledonian Railway Company made the purchase primarily to acquire Grangemouth Harbour as a distribution centre for their railway goods traffic, notably coal, rather than to strangle competition from the canal. In fact the Caledonian Railway Company had an incentive to continue investment in the canal, as it was still relatively successful and drew some trade away from the rival North British Railway Company, which operated the Edinburgh to Glasgow line. However, despite the Caledonian Railway Company's heavy expenditure on Grangemouth Harbour, and to a lesser degree on the canal itself, traffic and revenues declined steadily until the First World War. From about 1900 it was operating at a loss.[26] The main reason for the decline was the dominance of the

The Opening of Bonnybridge Bridge, Forth and Clyde Canal, 1900 ←
Falkirk Archives

Until 1900 the only connection between north and south Bonnybridge was a road under the canal, which was often flooded. This view shows the opening ceremony for the new bascule bridge to link the two parts of the town.

Midget Submarine 'Shrimp' on the Forth and Clyde Canal →
Scotsman Publications

In 1957 midget submarine XE14, 'Shrimp' commanded by Lt W. Ricketts travelled through the canal from the Clyde to Rosyth on the Forth to be decommissioned. It is seen here at Knightswood Lock.

Telfer Drummond, 'Two Horse Power', about 1930 ←
Falkirk Archives

A barge being pulled by a pair of horses, on the Forth and Clyde Canal. The barge is laden with logs.

Maryhill Road Aqueduct with Sailing Boat and Tram, 1961 →
Newsquest (Herald & Times)

By 1881, Robert Whitworth's original aqueduct, over what was then Wyndford Street, had become an obstruction to traffic. The new aqueduct was built in that year. This image shows an electric tram in the last full year of operation before the closure of the Glasgow trams in 1962.

Speirs Wharf, Maryhill Motorway Proposals
Alexander D. Bell

The canal at Speirs Wharf was considered for infilling to form part of the proposed Maryhill Motorway in 1975. This artist's impression shows the impressive range of warehouses retained along the side of the motorway. Strathclyde Regional Council eventually abandoned the scheme in the late 1970s.

railways, particularly the North British Railway, which developed its network to include mineral and goods lines and provided access to markets across mainland Britain without the need for transhipment. As old industries died, new ones looked to convenient sites away from the canal and near to the railways. Additionally, the dimensions of the canal proved increasingly inadequate for transporting the raw materials, industrial products and passenger steamers of the late nineteenth century.

The closure of the docks at Grangemouth to merchant traffic during the First World War, the advent of motorised road transport, and the Great Depression of the 1930s all contributed to the falling-off in use of the canal and its subsequent decay. Pleasure craft continued to use the canal until 1939, and small fishing vessels used the route into the 1960s to move between the east and west coasts, but the movement of goods was negligible. Along with the railways and other functioning canals, the Forth and Clyde Canal was nationalised and placed under the control of the British Transport Commission after the Second World War. The Clyde Valley Regional Plan of 1946 noted the canal as 'a disadvantage to development and an obstruction to road and rail communications'

and recommended that it would 'be in the public interest for this canal to be discontinued and filled in'.[27] Low usage, maintenance costs, high numbers of accidental drownings and continued pressure for removal of the constraints on development and the road and rail networks led to closure of the canal on 1 January 1963 under the Forth and Clyde Canal (Extinguishment of Rights of Navigation) Act 1962.[28] Subsequently, many locks and bridges fell into disrepair and the canal became silted and clogged with rubbish in places. In numerous locations, new road bridges, utility services and infilling completely blocked the canal, most significantly at Grangemouth and Clydebank.

RENAISSANCE, 1971–PRESENT DAY

In 1971, within just nine years of the closure, various local authorities along the route were at work on finding a new future for the canal. The Inland Waterways Amenity Advisory Council, statutory advisers to the Secretary of State for the Environment and the British Waterways Board, delivered a report in 1974 regretting the 'short sighted thinking' and 'premature decision' to close the canal, and presented a strong argument for reopening both the Forth and Clyde Canal and the

Speirs Wharf, Forth and Clyde Canal

Nick Haynes

The buildings at Speirs Wharf were once central to Glasgow's industrial development housing grain mills, a sugar refinery and warehouses. As part of the ongoing regeneration of the canal, they have been developed into flats and office space.

Union Canal.[29] As a result of further community pressure and encouragement by voluntary bodies such as the Scottish Inland Waterways Association, Strathclyde Regional Council recommended rehabilitation of the canal as a recreational amenity in its Regional Plan of 1976.[30] Local authorities along the canal set up a study group in 1977, which produced a survey report in 1979.[31] The Forth and Clyde Canal Society was formed in 1980, raising public awareness, encouraging restoration projects, organising events and eventually running boats. A major turning point in the regeneration of the Glasgow branch of the canal was the 1985–92 refurbishment and conversion to housing of the impressive range of mills and warehouses at Speirs Wharf in Glasgow by developer Windex Limited with substantial government financial support through the Scottish Development Agency and Historic Scotland. Adoption of the Forth and Clyde Canal Local Plan in 1988 gave formal recognition to the aims of promoting and increasing recreational use, maximising the available lengths of water, and protecting the canal from further obstructions.

The creation of the National Lottery and Millennium Commission in 1994 enabled British Waterways and numerous funding partners

to promote an ambitious £84.5m scheme, the Millennium Link, to reopen the Forth and Clyde Canal from Grangemouth to Bowling and the Union Canal from Edinburgh to Falkirk, and to reinstate the link between the canals. Work began on site in March 1999 to repair or rebuild bridges to meet modern standards and road alignments, construct new bridges, repair or rebuild locks, dredge the canal to a depth of six feet, eliminate pollutants and remove all obstructions to navigation.[32] The largest of these obstacles on the Forth and Clyde Canal was the loss of the two mile connection through Grangemouth to the docks and River Forth, which was overcome by the construction of a new 776-yard length of canal, a mooring basin and two locks feeding into a newly dredged section of the River Carron. The Forth and Clyde Canal reopened for navigation from end to end on 26 May 2001.[33] The Millennium Link project was enormously successful in stimulating awareness of the canal, further improvements, new leisure uses and attracting regeneration of surrounding areas. The Glasgow Canal Regeneration Partnership, formed by Scottish Canals, Glasgow City Council, ISIS developers and Igloo Regeneration Fund in 2004 has been instrumental in promoting the

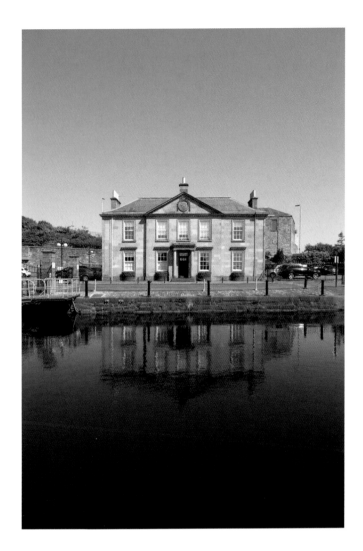

canal as a focus for regeneration of the deprived areas, derelict buildings and contaminated former industrial lands that line its route through the city. Some of the many improvements include: the construction of a new canal link and locks between Speirs Wharf and Pinkston Basin at Port Dundas in 2006; the conversion of the former Highland Distilleries bonded warehouse at Speirs Locks to workshops and offices for the creative industries; the development of Pinkston Basin in Port Dundas as Scotland's first purpose-built urban watersports centre; and the creation of a new urban village at Maryhill Locks.[34] At the time of writing a masterplan has been completed for a cultural quarter to the west of Speirs Locks and a masterplan is in progress for the former Diageo site at Port Dundas, both with the aim of bringing sustainable vitality, jobs and investment to the canalside and its communities.

Regeneration has not been restricted to Glasgow, with investment in repairs and improvements continuing along the length of the canal.

Canal House, Speirs Wharf
Nick Haynes

Canal House is an attractive two-storied Georgian building originally constructed as offices for the Forth and Clyde Canal Company in 1812. The building was restored in 1989.

Conservation Work at Craigmarloch Stables
Peter Sandground

Like a number of the 'horse barracks', or stables, along the canal, Craigmarloch had fallen into disrepair by the 1980s. This image records maintenance and archaeological work in progress as part of the canal college in 2014. Run by the Scottish Waterways Trust and supported by Scottish Canals, canal college is a training programme for 16 to 25-year-olds that teaches heritage, environment and employability skills on the Lowland Canals and at the Falkirk Wheel.

Lambhill Stables, Forth and Clyde Canal
Nick Haynes

Lambhill Stables were constructed in about 1820 to a standard design of ground floor stables with hayloft above. Similar blocks were located along the canal at regular intervals of four miles to service the horses that pulled the new 'Swift' passenger boats. The building fell into dereliction in the 1960s, but was refurbished in 2011 to form a community hub.

The Kelpies under Construction

Peter Sandground

Construction of The Kelpies began on 17 June 2013. In a monumental feat of engineering, The Kelpies rose from the ground in just ninety days. Designed by Scottish sculptor, Andy Scott, the enormous sculptures were manufactured and installed by SH Structures Limited. The horses rise up to ninety-eight feet high and each weighs 300 tonnes. Towering above the Forth and Clyde Canal, The Kelpies are the centrepiece of Scotland's newest parkland at The Helix, which lies between Falkirk and Grangemouth in the Forth Valley.

Auchinstarry Basin was redeveloped as a marina and activity centre in 2004–5.[35] Even after the Millennium Link project the sea-lock connection to the River Forth at Grangemouth remained problematic, as the thirteen feet to sixteen-and-a-half feet tidal range of the River Carron left boats struggling to get underneath the nearby bridge at high tide and without enough water to float at low tide. In 2006, the Helix Trust began to develop plans for an £13.4m, 766-yard, northwards extension to a new sea lock as part of a larger regeneration project for Helix Park. Without doubt the most spectacular elements of the canal extension scheme, opened in 2014, are Andy Scott's two ninety-eight-foot high stainless steel sculpted heads of the Kelpies, mythical water creatures that can take the form of horses. A masterplan has been prepared for Port Downie, near Falkirk, and the 2014 conversion to retail and leisure units of the railway arches at Bowling Basin marks the first stage of a £1m investment programme in the canal's western gateway, where a masterplan is also in progress.

Monkland Canal

Monkland Canal

Keith Fergus / Scottish Viewpoint

The Monkland Canal is no longer available for navigation but is still a vital part of Scotland's canal system, providing the main water supply to the Forth and Clyde Canal. Built in 1790–4 to the designs of James Watt, the canal brought much needed cheap supplies of coal into the burgeoning town of Glasgow and accelerated the development of other industries such as iron-working in the Lanarkshire hills.

I somehow or other got into the good graces of our present magistracy [Glasgow Town Council], who have employed me in engineering for them (as Mr. Smeaton terms it); among other things I have projected a canal to bring coals to the town; for though coal is everywhere hereabout in plenty and the very town stands upon it, yet measures have been taken by industrious people to monopolize it and raise its price 50 per cent. within these ten years. Now this canal is nine miles long, goes to a country full of level free coals of good quality, in the hands of many proprietors, who sell them at present at 6d. per cart of 7cwt. at the pit. There is a valley from Glasgow to the place, but it has a rise of 266 feet perpendicular above our river; I therefore set that aside, and have found among the hills a passage, whereby a canal may come within a mile of the town without locks, from whence the coals can be brought on a waggon-way. This canal will cost 10,000l. [£10,000] – is proposed 16 feet wide at bottom, the boats 9 feet wide and 50 feet long, to draw 21/2 feet water.

Letter from James Watt to Dr William Small, 12 December 1769.[1]

Officially abandoned in 1950, and partly culverted and obliterated from view during construction of the M8 motorway in the 1970s, the Monkland Canal is now difficult to envisage as early nineteenth-century Scotland's busiest and most commercially successful canal. Although the Monkland Canal is still the principal water supply to the Forth and Clyde Canal, much of the western end of the main canal is now channelled through underground pipes, and only two water-filled sections at the eastern end survive as linear parks from the North Calder Water to Carnbroe at Coatbridge and from Blair Road to Cuilhill. A short section of the Gartsherrie Branch has also been revived as part of the Museum of Scottish Industrial Life on the site of the Summerlee Ironworks.

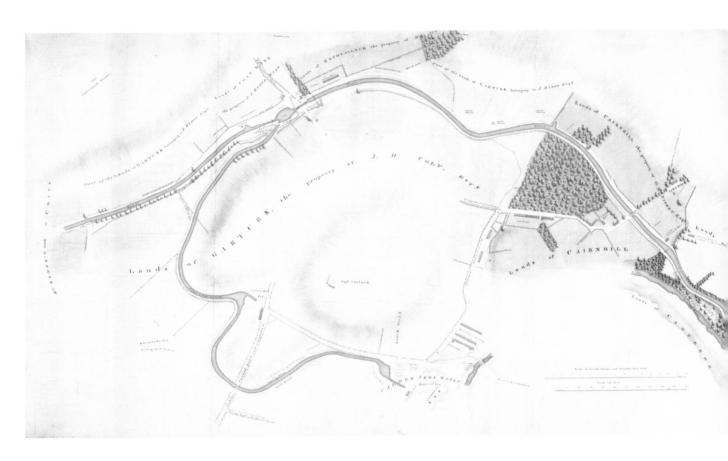

PLANNING THE CANAL, 1769–70

Unlike the Forth and Clyde Canal, which was regarded as a national strategic asset for general purposes, the original nine miles of the Monkland Canal were conceived for a very specific commercial reason, to break the local monopoly on coal supplies to the city of Glasgow. The Trades House of Glasgow laid the blame for the exorbitant price of coal in the city on the 'arts and methods' of the Rae family, who had opened their coal mine at Little Govan in 1743.[2] Apart from the sharp practices of the coalmasters, the small number of suppliers and the rapidly increasing industry and population of the city were undoubtedly further factors in Glasgow's fuel poverty crisis of the 1750s and 60s. The town council considered numerous proposals to deal with the problem, but the 1768 election of James Buchanan of Drumpellier (in the parish of Old Monkland) to the office of Lord Provost of Glasgow, stimulated an ambitious plan to open up the Monkland coalfields by means of a new canal to the city. The rich coalfields were largely unexploited and in the hands of numerous proprietors, who it was hoped would compete with each other to undercut the city's existing suppliers.

Glasgow Town Council commissioned the inventor, scientist, engineer and polymath, James Watt, to survey the ground between the city and the coalfields. In order to fund his family life and sustain his steam engine experiments, Watt had maintained his scientific instrument-making business and was working as a surveyor on canal and river navigation projects for various clients, including the town council and the trustees of the Forfeited Estates. He completed his Monkland canal study in November 1769 and presented options for two routes.[3] The first option, at an estimated cost of £20,317, involved twenty-five locks and a direct route from the east

Map of the Eastern End of the Monkland Canal, 1822
Scottish Canals

The Monkland Canal was twelve miles long and designed to bring coal from the mining areas of Monklands to Glasgow. In the course of a long and difficult construction process, it was opened progressively as sections were completed, from 1771. It reached Gartcraig in 1782, and in 1794 it reached its full originally planned extent, from pits at Calderbank to a basin at Townhead in Glasgow; at first this was in two sections with a ninety-six foot vertical interval between them at Blackhill; coal was unloaded and carted to the lower section and loaded onto a fresh barge. Locks were later constructed linking the two sections, and the canal was also connected to the Forth and Clyde Canal, providing additional business potential.

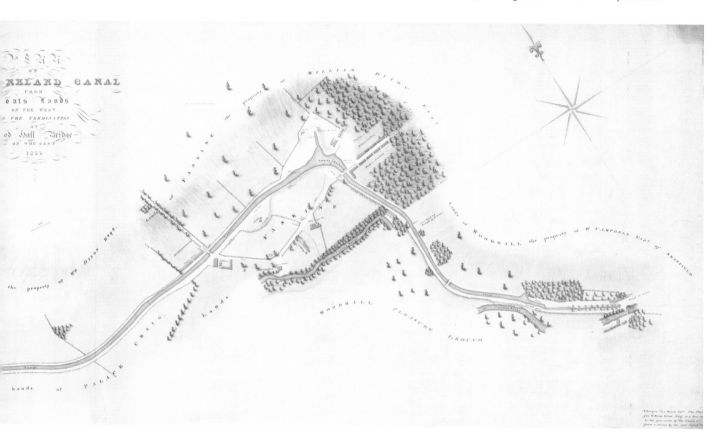

side of Coatbridge via Barrachnie, Shettleston, Camlachie and Glasgow Green, entering the River Clyde below the modern-day Albert Bridge. The second proposal took a meandering, but level and lock-less, route from Coatbridge via Cuilhill, Easterhouse, Milncroft, Gartcraig, Smithycroft, Provanmill and terminating at Germiston. Here the coals would be transferred to carts and a wagon-way would negotiate the steep slope down into the city centre. It was this second proposal without locks, estimated at £9,653, that the organising committee selected on the 3 January 1770.[4]

Following selection of a route, progress was swift. Subscribers to the £100 shares of the 'Company of Proprietors of the Monkland Navigation' included the owners of the Monkland coalfields, a number of Glasgow's tobacco lords and merchants, and several public bodies and institutions, such as the town council, the Trades House, the University and the incorporations of masons, wrights, bakers, maltmen and fleshers.[5] The town council promoted 'An Act for making and maintaining a navigable cut or canal, and waggon-way, from the collieries in the parishes of Old and New Monkland, to the city of Glasgow', which was granted royal assent on 12 April 1770.[6] The preamble to the Act set out a number of objectives for the canal, including the reduction of coal prices for the advantage of the trade and manufacturers of Glasgow, the relief of the poor, the preservation of public roads, and improvement of the surrounding lands.

BUILDING THE CANAL, 1770–94

Watt was appointed chief engineer on a salary of £200 per year, and the company ordered work to start at the eastern end of the route on 20 May 1770.[7] At John Smeaton's suggestion in

John Partridge, after Sir William Beechey,
Portrait of James Watt
Scottish National Portrait Gallery, Edinburgh

James Watt (1736–1819) was an inventor and mechanical engineer whose improvements in steam engine technology drove the Industrial Revolution. Born in Greenock he went to London as an apprentice scientific instrument maker. On his return to Glasgow, and still only nineteen, he set up his own business. He was soon recognised as an exceptional engineer, and employed on the Monkland Canal and surveys of other canals. He was also involved in the deepening of Scottish rivers, including the River Clyde.

July 1770, the canal was deepened to four feet from the original three feet by building up the banks. In spite of problems controlling the quality of work by contractors, four miles were cut by September 1771 and seven miles completed in November 1772.[8] Some of the other practical difficulties of managing the project are revealed in a letter from Watt to his friend William Small:

Our whole expense, act, surveys, &c., will be about 10,000l. spent. I have surveyed, levelled, planned, staked out, and measured the cube yards cut, of the whole, personally; I have also made bargains, superintended the work and accounts, and by myself and one clerk paid the cash. I have to the bargain been obliged to oversee every piece of work that was in the least out of the common road. I am now, in spite of a most [inclement] season, from five to six hours in the fields every day, and ride about ten miles. This is the one side. On the other, I am extremely indolent, cannot force workmen to do their duty, have been cheated by undertakers [contractors] and clerks, and am unlucky enough to know it. The work done is slovenly, our workmen are bad, and I am not sufficiently strict. I am happy in the friendship of the principal residing proprietors, and am welcome to their houses as to my own, otherwise my wretched health could not have borne the fatigues I have undergone.[9]

However, it was financial, rather than physical, distress that brought work on the project to a halt at Barlinnie, some two miles short of its intended destination at Germiston, in December 1772. The cost of land had been higher than anticipated, an additional foot of depth was added to the channel at the outset of construction without revising the costs, the ground proved tougher than expected (particularly Drumpellier Moss and the cut through the hill at Muttonhole), the weather caused delays, and a tunnel over a burn collapsed, requiring repairs and further expense. The failure of the Ayr Bank in June 1772 and the subsequent credit crisis had an enormous impact on the economy of Scotland, and in particular on large infrastructure and

Blackhill Locks and Incline View, Monkland Canal →
Scottish Canals

In the early days the main purpose of the canal was to supply coal to Glasgow, but from the 1830s the new traffic in iron put pressure on capacity. The first measures to increase reliability and capacity were to add a new set of locks in parallel to the existing decayed locks, then to rebuild the old locks. The top drawing opposite by John Macneill, a protégé of Thomas Telford and later regarded as the father of the Irish railway system, shows designs of 1837 for a replacement lock at Blackhill. The new locks were built under the supervision of the Glasgow engineer Andrew Thompson. The drawing below of 1839 by James Leslie shows a design for the second proposal to increase capacity: an inclined plane to haul up empty barges on their return journey from Glasgow. Two lines of rails were to be laid in a cutting and wheeled caissons (water-filled cradles) would operate up and down the one-in-ten gradient slope in balance. Eventually a modified system, known locally as the 'gazoon', was constructed with a steam winding-engine in 1850. It functioned successfully until 1887.

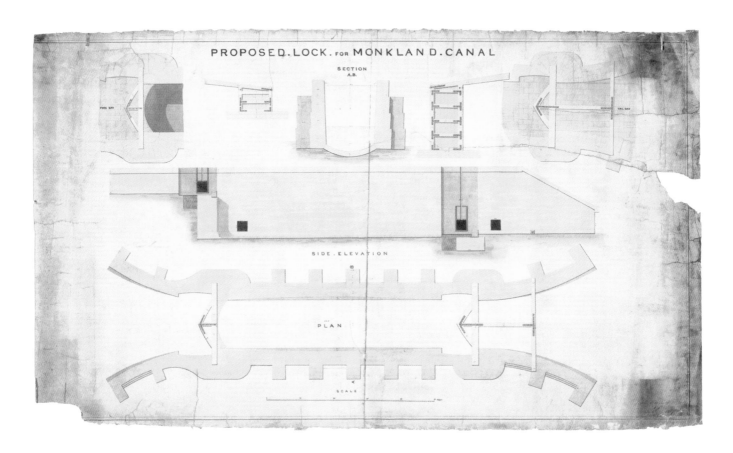

PROPOSED. LOCK. FOR MONKLAND. CANAL

SECTION
A.B.

FORE BAY

TAIL BAY

SIDE. ELEVATION

PLAN

SCALE

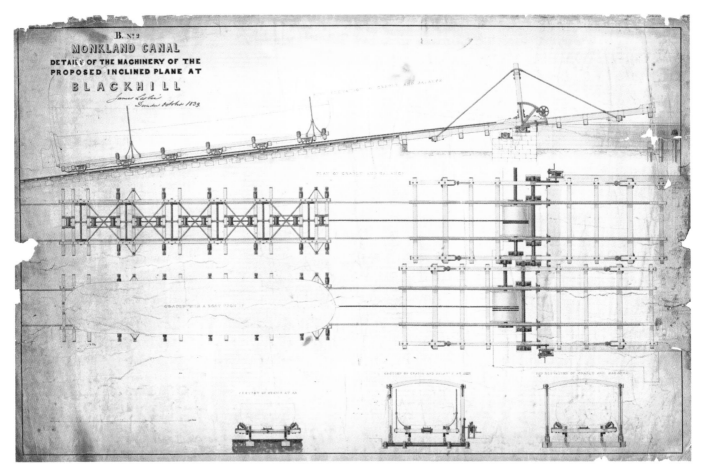

B. Nº 2

MONKLAND CANAL

DETAILS OF THE MACHINERY OF THE
PROPOSED INCLINED PLANE AT

BLACKHILL

James Hopkirk, View from the North of the Monkland Canal Basin at Castle Street
Glasgow University Library, Special Collections

Hopkirk's view from the canal basin at Castle Street shows Glasgow Cathedral, the Glasgow Royal Infirmary and the Knox Monument in the distance at the left of the picture. The Monkland Canal was opened from Monklands to Riddrie in 1773 and then to Blackhill in the 1780s when this basin was built. The distinctive building on the right is the Glasgow Royal Asylum designed by William Stark and built 1810–14.

Aerial View of Tennant's Chemical Works, St Rollox, Monkland Canal
RCAHMS

Charles Tennant's St Rollox Chemical Works was at one time the largest chemical manufacturer in the world. In 1964 it closed its plant to the east of Port Dundas. The M8 motorway was constructed immediately to the south, over the route of the Monkland Canal, in the 1970s, obstructing access to the canal basin.

development projects. As reported in the *Aberdeen Journal*: 'the new town between Edinburgh and Leith is suddenly stopped. In short, the same shock has been now given to Scotland as in King William's reign when the Darien Company was broke and the massacre of Glencoe happened'.[10] In view of the uncertain economic climate, there was unsurprisingly little enthusiasm amongst the Monkland Canal's backers to inject further significant investment. In any case, Watt believed that the section of canal from Coatbridge to Barlinnie was 'of immediate and profitable use because even from that termination we can afford to undersell others'.[11] Watt's optimism about the profitability of the incomplete canal proved unfounded. In debt and underused, the canal was sold by public auction on 14 August 1781.[12] The following year, ten new

proprietors began to extend the canal westwards from Barlinnie to Blackhill, where wagons would transfer coal down the steep slope to a separate cut of the canal that led to Castle Street at the head of Glasgow High Street. The additional sections, designed by new engineers, opened on 18 October 1784.[13] However, the wagon transfer remained a nuisance and an obstacle to use of the canal. By 1790 all the stock in the canal company had been acquired by Andrew Stirling of Drumpellier and the merchants William and George Stirling. The Stirlings invested in the Monkland Canal, promoting a new Act of Parliament to deepen it to four-and-a-half feet and extend it westwards to link with the Forth and Clyde Canal and eastwards via locks at Sheepford to meet the North Calder Water and, perhaps most importantly, added a flight of

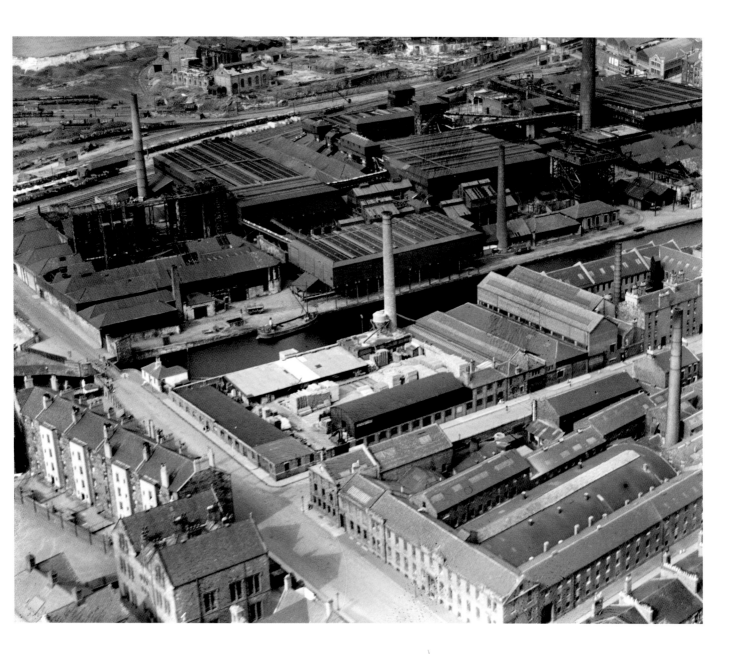

connecting locks and basins at Blackhill in 1793.[14] Apart from allowing through traffic, the connection to Port Dundas enabled the Monkland Canal to serve as a supply for the water-hungry locks of the Forth and Clyde Canal. The directors of the Forth and Clyde Canal strengthened this role in 1796–8 by building what was then the world's largest man-made reservoir near the source of the North Calder Water at Hillend, Caldercruix, which then fed through the Monkland Canal.

SUCCESSFUL OPERATION, 1790–1863

By 1793 there were four collieries along the line of the canal at Faskine, Barrachnie, Fullarton and Coats and Dundyvan. Finally the completed canal route broke the Glasgow coal monopoly by creating its own near-monopoly on the supply of Monkland

coal. The canal began to make money in the early years of the nineteenth century. Dividends were paid from 1807.[15] By 1817 the canal was twelve-and-a-quarter miles in length, had thirty-four bridges, and carried some 80,000 tons of coal annually at two pence per ton and 11,470 passengers at one shilling and sixpence for the cabin and one shilling steerage.[16] However, it was the exploitation of the Lanarkshire ironstone deposits and the phenomenally successful development of the iron industry in Coatbridge from 1825 onwards that brought a degree of financial stability to the canal.[17] Glasgow's entrepreneurial manufacturers created an insatiable demand for the products of the Monkland iron industries, which were sent by canal to the city for transformation from pig iron ingots into every conceivable size and shape of

View Looking South-east showing Part of
Gartsherrie Hornock and Summerlee Branch Canal
with Railway Bridge in Background
RCAHMS

This short one-mile branch canal was planned to serve
local coal mines, but by the time of its completion it
connected the newly-established Gartsherrie Iron
Works. Summerlee Iron Works was built on the same
branch in 1836.

finished goods. An expensive second staircase of locks and three new basins, built under the supervision of the Glasgow engineer, Andrew Thompson, were completed at Blackhill in 1841 to relieve the traffic.[18] These locks were augmented in 1850 by an 'inclined plane', designed by James Leslie of Leslie & Bateman Engineers, on which empty boats were steam-hauled up the 1-in-10 gradient of the hill in 'caissons' (water-filled cradles) on rails. This extraordinary water- and time-saving device, known locally as 'the gazoon', remained in service until 1887. A number of branches of the canal were built to service individual pits and ironworks including: Drumpellier; Gartsherrie, Hornock and Summerlee; Dundyvan; Langloan; Calder; and Bredisholm. In 1846 the Forth and Clyde Canal Company bought the Monkland Canal. At its height in 1863, the Monkland Canal held its own against the increasing competition from the railways by keeping prices low, carrying 1,529,918 tons of goods and generating £37,987 in revenue.[19]

DECLINE AND CLOSURE, 1863–1952

Within just five years of the purchase of the Forth and Clyde and Monkland Canals by the Caledonian Railway Company in 1867, the Monkland's annual tonnages and revenues had dropped by more than a third from their 1863 peak. The dramatic downward trend was to continue in both indicators towards the new century, when tonnages adopted a more gradual decline and revenues fluctuated between £2,000 and £1,000 until the 1920s. The canal fell out of use completely in the mid-1930s. The prime reasons for the decline of the Monkland Canal were the gradual exhaustion of the mineral and coalfields situated near the canal and the

Deterioration of Monkland Canal
Newsquest (Herald & Times) | RCAHMS

By 1935 the Monkland Canal had no commercial trade but its function as the water supply for the Forth and Clyde Canal and the Pinkston Power Station kept it from complete abandonment. Pressure to improve safety on the derelict canal resulted in Coatbridge Town Council filling-in sections of the canal. In the early 70s, during construction of the M8 motorway almost six miles of the watercourse were piped underground. These images show the dereliction of the Blackhill Locks and incline in the 1950s.

growth of competition from the railways. The relatively short route, concentration of successful heavy industrial concerns around the canal, minor passenger trade, early construction of side-cuts, basins and depots to service them, and initial lack of competing standard-gauge railways preserved the Monkland Canal in profit for a little longer than the Forth and Clyde Canal. However, the opening in 1870 of the Glasgow to Coatbridge branch of the North British Railway, which competed directly with the Monkland Canal and the railway interests of its owners, marked the beginning of the end for the canal. The iron trade moved to the railways and by 1906 had vanished forever from the canal. Coal from the diminishing number of canal-side pits continued to supply the Pinkston Power Station at Port Dundas into the 1920s, but by 1935 the canal had no commercial trade.

The Monkland Canal's function as a water supply to the Forth and Clyde Canal and to Pinkston Power Station kept it from complete abandonment until 1950.[20] By this time the 'nolly' (the local term for canal) had become a serious drowning hazard, earning its reputation as the 'killer canal' particularly at the Blackford Locks, where over a period of years many children lost their lives falling into the water from the top of the lock-gates.[21] At Coatbridge, the canal was thought to be the breeding ground for a plague of mosquitoes known as 'flying tigers'.[22] Certainly it was notorious for rats in places. The Clyde Valley Regional Plan of 1946 described the canal in mixed terms: 'Over considerable stretches the amenities are pleasant; it can be claimed that certain portions of the disused tow-path provide a popular walk. At other locations as, for instance, in passing through Coatbridge, the disused canal is alike an obstruction to development and a source of nuisance.'[23] Pressure to improve the safety of the derelict canal resulted in the removal of the Castle Street basin and Blackford Locks and piping of the water in 1954. In 1963 Coatbridge Town Council began the decade-long project of filling in sections of the canal through the town centre. Almost six miles

Bank Street Basin, Monkland Canal
RCAHMS

Aerial view of the canal basin showing the refurbishment
of the Summerlee Museum of Scottish Industrial Life
within the former Hydrocon Crane Works in 2007.

of the watercourse were also piped underground
in the early 1970s during construction of the M8,
or 'Monkland Motorway', along the canal corridor
between Townhead and Easterhouse.

RENAISSANCE, 1975–PRESENT DAY

With the opening of Stage 1 (Townhead to
Cumbernauld Road) of the Monkland Motorway
in May 1975 came an increasing concern to retain
and reuse the surviving sections of open water as
amenity and natural heritage corridors. Stages 2A
(A80 to Stepps Road) and 2B (Steppes Road to
the city boundary) of the motorway were already at
an advanced stage of planning, but the Monkland
Canal Land Renewal Project sought to develop a
network of walkways along the canal corridor to the
east, and to return some sections to a navigable

Summerlee Museum of Scottish Industrial Life, Monkland Canal

Nick Haynes

Summerlee Museum was opened in 1987 to interpret the social and industrial history of Central Scotland, in particular the Monklands area. It was built on one of Scotland's most important ironworks and the remains of its blast furnaces and other buildings can still be seen from parts of the museum.

state. There are now two stretches of open water between Woodside Drive, Calderbank and Paddock Street, Coatbridge and through Drumpellier Country Park between Blair Road, Coatbridge and Cuilhill Road, and part of the National Cycle Route 75 runs from Coatbridge to Bargeddie along the route of the canal. The development from 1984 of the Summerlee Heritage Park, now known as Summerlee Museum of Scottish Industrial Life, on the old Summerlee Ironworks site enabled the reopening of Howes Basin and a short section of the Gartsherrie branch of the canal. There are walks along the North Calder Water to Hillend Reservoir, which still supplies the Monkland Canal and the Forth and Clyde Canal.

The Monkland Canal Development Framework of 2009 analysed the canal corridor for improvement opportunities, which led to a number of projects to enhance the legibility, accessibility and amenity of the route, for example at Blair Bridge, where a new gateway designed by Andy Scott celebrates the work of local comic book writer, Mark Millar, and marks the beginning of the open water to the west of Coatbridge. The 2010 refurbishment of the site of the old Bank Street Basin created a new public open space for Coatbridge and reconnected pedestrian links between the town's visitor attractions, the town centre and local facilities.

Vulcan
Nick Haynes

The steam barge 'Vulcan', the first iron-hulled boat in Scotland, was constructed in 1819 at Faskine on the Monkland Canal by Monklands Ironworks. A replica of the original 'Vulcan' built at Govan by apprentices of British Shipbuilders Training Ltd is now at Summerlee Museum of Scottish Industrial Life.

Bank Street Basin, Coatbridge, Monkland Canal
Nick Haynes

The renaissance of the Monkland Canal, which began in 2008, is led by Scottish Canals, the Scottish Waterways Trust, North Lanarkshire Council, Summerlee Museum of Scottish Industrial Life, Sustrans and Calderbank Conservation Society. Bank Street Basin was redesigned by Paul Hogarth Company Ltd in 2010.

Andy Scott's Blair Road Gateway, Coatbridge, Monkland Canal
Nick Haynes

The Blair Bridge Gateway Project is part of a raft of new landscaping and access improvements which, together, create a new gateway to the two-hundred-year-old Monkland Canal and improve the mile and a half stretch of canal between Blair Bridge and Bargeddie. The project consists of a new entrance gateway, environmental improvements, access improvements and interpretive signage. North Lanarkshire Council's Landscape Services designed the landscape improvement programme to raise the quality and feel of the area from an uncared for wasteland into an inspiring and inviting entrance. The new six metre high sculptural steel archway was created by renowned Scottish artist Andy Scott in 2011.

Crinan Canal

Crinan Canal
D. Habron / Scottish Viewpoint

Known as 'the most beautiful shortcut in the world', construction of the Crinan Canal began in 1794 under the supervision of consultant engineer John Rennie, but, although it opened in 1801, it was only finally completed in 1809. It was built to avoid the arduous route around the Mull of Kintyre to and from the Western Isles. The Crinan is only nine miles in length and is set in one of the most stunning natural landscapes in Scotland.

... the expediency of a shorter navigation between the Atlantic and the Clyde must appear obvious to every observer. It is a matter not only of national utility, but of moral obligation. It touches the feelings of humanity, and calls loudly for immediate redress... A voyage which frequently takes 3 weeks, would by this easy passage, be performed in 3 or 4 days, in all seasons of the year, whether in time of war or peace. By cutting off the peninsula of Cantire [Kintyre], the voyage from Glasgow to the Hebrides would be intirely inland, and thereby screened in a great measure from the dreadful tempests of the Atlantic.

John Knox, 1784[1]

The Crinan Canal is a nine-mile ship canal, connecting the Firth of Clyde with the Sound of Jura, the Inner Hebrides and the West Highlands, without the need to navigate the exposed and treacherous Mull of Kintyre. Often described as 'one of the world's most beautiful short-cuts', the route also forms part of the link between the western ends of the Forth and Clyde Canal and the Caledonian Canal. The dimensions of the canal vary through its three reaches or sections (east, summit and west) with the depth ranging between twelve feet and fifteen feet and the surface width between forty feet and ninety feet.[2] There are fifteen locks, including two sea locks. The eight eastern locks raise the canal to its summit between Cairnbaan and Dunardry, sixty-three feet above sea level, and the seven western locks lower it back to the level of Loch Crinan. The short half-mile length of the summit reach was to cause problems in maintaining a water supply to the locks on either side. Six swing bridges and one retractable bridge cross the canal, all of which are replacements for earlier structures.

PLANNING THE CANAL, 1730–1793
Like many of the other Scottish canal schemes of the late eighteenth century, the Crinan Canal had a long gestation. Even before 1730 Alexander Gordon had suggested 'it deserves Enquiry if the small

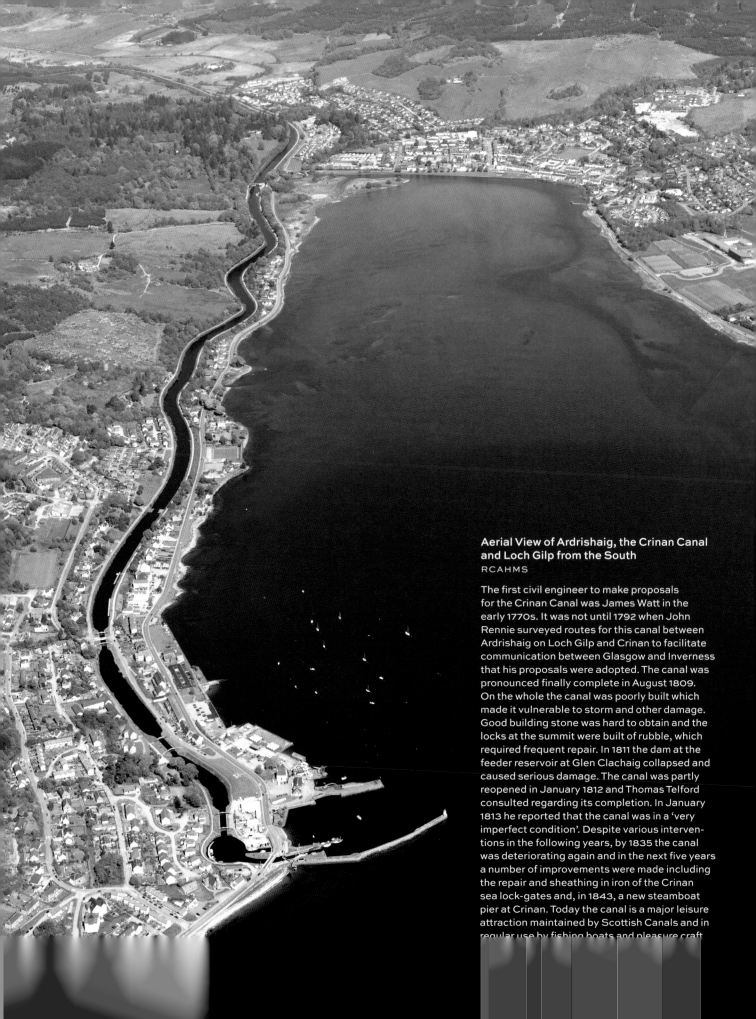

Aerial View of Ardrishaig, the Crinan Canal and Loch Gilp from the South
RCAHMS

The first civil engineer to make proposals for the Crinan Canal was James Watt in the early 1770s. It was not until 1792 when John Rennie surveyed routes for this canal between Ardrishaig on Loch Gilp and Crinan to facilitate communication between Glasgow and Inverness that his proposals were adopted. The canal was pronounced finally complete in August 1809. On the whole the canal was poorly built which made it vulnerable to storm and other damage. Good building stone was hard to obtain and the locks at the summit were built of rubble, which required frequent repair. In 1811 the dam at the feeder reservoir at Glen Clachaig collapsed and caused serious damage. The canal was partly reopened in January 1812 and Thomas Telford consulted regarding its completion. In January 1813 he reported that the canal was in a 'very imperfect condition'. Despite various interventions in the following years, by 1835 the canal was deteriorating again and in the next five years a number of improvements were made including the repair and sheathing in iron of the Crinan sea lock-gates and, in 1843, a new steamboat pier at Crinan. Today the canal is a major leisure attraction maintained by Scottish Canals and in regular use by fishing boats and pleasure craft.

Portrait of John Rennie by Sir Henry Raeburn
about 1810
Scottish National Portrait Gallery, Edinburgh

John Rennie (1761–1821) was a prolific engineer, from the heroic age of canal construction. The waterways he built include the Crinan Canal, the Kennet and Avon Canal and the Rochdale Canal. These canals brought about unprecedented changes in Britain's industry, allowing goods and raw materials to be transported around the country. Rennie's work on canals, aqueducts, bridges and canals mark him as one of the greatest engineers of his age.

Isthmus in Kentire [between East Loch Tarbert and West Loch Tarbert] could be safely cut, which if Effected would be of Great Importance to Trade and Navigation particularly for Herring Fishing'.[3] The short isthmus at Tarbert was still under consideration when James Watt undertook a study of potential canal routes for the Board of Trustees for the Forfeited Annexed Estates in 1771.[4] Although the east-west Loch Tarbert route would have required the shortest canal, the longer and more expensive Loch Gilp to Loch Crinan route allowed a safer journey with less exposure to open sea.

The trustees for the Forfeited Annexed Estates took no further action on Watt's plans. However, the idea was kept alive in various proposals to bring industry and 'improvement' to the impoverished inhabitants of the Highlands and Islands after the subsistence crisis of 1782–3. Two of the main proponents of a Crinan canal were the bitter rivals John Knox and James Anderson, who both gave evidence in its favour to a parliamentary select committee on fisheries in 1785.[5] The main point of difference between the two men was on the means of financing the canal while Knox proposed a mixture of public and private funding, Anderson insisted that the scheme should be a private initiative. The Highland Society of Edinburgh, formed in 1784, and the British Fisheries Society, incorporated by Act of Parliament in 1786, also took an active interest in the promotion of a canal. It was the president and vice-president of this latter society, John Campbell, 5th Duke of Argyll, and John Campbell, 4th Earl of Breadalbane and Holland, who finally commissioned John Rennie to make a survey of potential canal routes between Loch Gilp and Loch Crinan in 1792.

Rennie proposed a single route from Ardrishaig to just east of Cairnbaan, and two options to complete the passage to Loch Crinan: one via Auchinshellach and the Moss of Crinan ending at Duntrune Castle; the other via Daill (then known as Dell) and Dunardry terminating at Crinan (formerly Port Righ or Portree) village. Harbours were projected at both ends of the canal. The promoters began preparations in London for a parliamentary bill on 27 June 1782 and opened subscriptions to the canal on 16 October.[6] The prospectus for the canal emphasised the numerous other trading and strategic benefits of the scheme, including: expansion of the local fisheries and industries including kelp (for glass and soap), slates, marble, sand, limestone, lead and agricultural produce; increased supply of salt for preserving the herring catch; supply of goods to and from Glasgow and the industrialised towns of the River Clyde; easy access for the herring fleet to the fishing grounds on either coast of the Kintyre and Knapdale Peninsulas; safe harbours and passages for trading vessels to the Atlantic, and the trade routes to the Baltic, the Americas and West Indies; reduced insurance for cargoes; introducing a 'spirit of enterprise' to the West Coast; generally improving local living conditions; and 'affording an additional source of wealth and force to the British Empire'.[7] The initial aim was to avoid 'an indolent dependence on the aid of government to public works', meeting the estimated £63,628 cost of construction through private subscription.[8] Apart from the canal dues, the promoters expected a return to landowning investors through general increased land and rental values on the West Coast.

Royal Assent was granted to 'An Act for making and maintaining a Navigable Canal from Loch Gilp to Loch Crinan in the Shire of Argyll' in May 1793, incorporating the Crinan Canal Company and authorising a maximum capital of £120,000 in £50 shares. By this time Rennie had surveyed

the route options in more detail, increased the proposed depth from twelve feet to fifteen feet, added two further locks, and revised the estimated costs to £107,512.[9] The involvement of the Duke of Argyll, who was elected governor of the new canal company, and the Earl of Breadalbane, ensured a range of influential aristocratic and entrepreneurial shareholders including the Marquess of Tweedale as well as Josiah Wedgwood, Glasgow Town Council, Glasgow Chamber of Commerce, and John Rennie himself. Four-fifths of the total subscribed was said to have derived from English investors.[10] A canal office was established at Inveraray and wharves at Loch Crinan and Loch Gilp in 1793 and construction work, aided by a steam engine, began at the Ardrishaig end on 30 June 1794.[11]

BUILDING THE CANAL, 1794–1817

The project was let to contractors in parcels and supervised by the resident engineer, John Paterson, and by Rennie on occasional trips north from his London base in Stamford Street.[12] Construction started well, but difficult ground (alternating soft moss and hard whinstone), short-ages of labour, lack of transport for the stone, and reluctant landowners slowed progress. By 1799, some three years after the original estimated completion date, five locks still remained to be constructed and rising prices and the high level of defaulting subscribers forced the canal company

Passage of Her Majesty Queen Victoria on the Crinan Canal
Private Collection

Queen Victoria travelled along the canal during a holiday in the Scottish Highlands in 1847. She made the journey on the barge 'Sunbeam' which had been specially fitted out and brought to the canal for the occasion. It was towed by four horses, two of which were ridden by postilions in royal livery. 'We glided along smoothly, and the views…were very fine … ' she recorded in her Journal, 'but the eleven locks we had to go through – (a very curious process, first passing several by rising, and then others by going down) – were tedious … ' At Crinan she boarded the royal yacht 'Victoria and Albert'. Her journey made the canal a tourist attraction and gave the canal an added purpose. Passenger steamer companies operating out of Glasgow advertised the canal as the 'Royal route' and by the late 1850s more than 40,000 passengers passed through Ardrishaig each year.

Views of the 'Linnet' Steamship (top) and the 'Chevalier' paddlesteamer (bottom) at Crinan Harbour
RCAHMS

In 1839 horse-drawn passage boats were introduced on the canal which were popular with holiday passengers who took the boats from Ardrishaig to connect with the northbound paddlesteamer 'Chevalier' waiting at Crinan. In 1866 the passage boats were replaced by the steamship 'Linnet', which carried mail in addition to other traffic. It was first operated, like many other steamers on the West Coast, by David Hutcheson & Co. From 1879 it was taken over by one of the former partners in that firm under his own name, David MacBrayne. 'Linnet' remained in service until 1929.

Puffers in the Canal Basin, Crinan Canal
RCAHMS

The Puffer is essentially a type of small steamboat which provided a vital supply link around the west coast and Hebridean islands of Scotland. These stumpy little cargo ships have achieved almost mythical status thanks largely to the short stories Neil Munro wrote about the 'Vital Spark' and her captain Para Handy. The Crinan Canal was extensively used by Puffers carrying coal and other goods until the 1960s. Although the canal basin is used now mainly by pleasure craft, it is also used by fishing boats and is a base for the 'VIC' 32', a Puffer converted to carry passengers.

Oakfield Bridge House, Crinan Canal
Peter Sandground

Scottish Canals has been working hard to restore a number of canal-side heritage properties. Central to this project is to attract third party funding to facilitate a sensitive restoration of key historic buildings and bring them back into productive use as high quality holiday accomodation. This approach secures the long-term future of the structures and by retaining them in public ownership enables a wide audience to enjoy the special qualities of these buildings and their relationship with the canal.

Harbour House, Crinan Canal
Peter Sandground

Built during the early development of the canal between 1794 and 1820, the former Harbour House and Post Office is located at the canal basin in the picturesque village of Crinan. It is a significant part of the early infrastructure of the canal. Harbour House with its tall and narrow chimney-stacks and steeply pitched piended roof was built into the bank of the canal basin. Siting the former post office beside the canal basin allowed for easy loading of mail onto the canal boats improving the efficiency of the postal service that operated through the canal.

to seek parliamentary approval to raise a further £30,000.[13] The Forth and Clyde Canal Company repaid their £50,000 government loan in June 1799, giving the treasury confidence to authorise the Barons of the Court of Exchequer to lend £25,000 of that repayment to the Crinan Canal Company with a mortgage over the canal.[14] After much difficulty in recruiting to such a remote location, the workforce reached its peak at 507 men in June 1800.[15] A further £9,810 was raised by another round of subscriptions in May 1801 and the canal was filled to a depth of eight feet. The first boat passed through the incomplete canal on 27 July 1801.[16] Another £25,000 government loan in 1804 enabled work to continue.

Financial and structural problems continued to dog the canal beyond its formal completion in August 1809.[17] The unexpected hardness and difficulty of cutting the whinstone caused the company to leave the western reach narrower than planned and with jagged sides in places, which resulted in numerous accidents. When the channel was cleared in 1878, some fifteen tons of broken propellers were recovered from this reach.[18] The sea entrances were too shallow, the bends on the western reach were too sharp and close together, some of the drawbridges were dangerous and several locks were leaky. Water was also a problem, usually from a lack of supply in the summer, but inundations caused collapses of the banks at Oakfield Moss in 1805 and of the Glen Clachaig reservoir dam in 1811. Only three years after its completion, the canal was in such a poor state that Thomas Telford was commissioned to report on necessary repairs and improvements. These were duly undertaken in 1816–17 using a third government loan of £19,400. The canal reopened on 20 November 1817. By this time, the heavily mortgaged canal was vested in the Barons of the Exchequer in Edinburgh and its management placed with the Commissioners of the Caledonian Canal.

FLUCTUATING FORTUNES, 1817–1980s

The canal operated reasonably successfully in the early 1820s, to the extent that it covered its operating and maintenance costs, but not the servicing of its debts. Trade was volatile in the transport of fish, slates and kelp, but the new steamboats were successful, carrying almost 14,000 passengers in 1827.[19] In spite of various attempts by the canal company to regain control of the Crinan Canal, it became increasingly clear that the original proprietors were incapable of raising sufficient capital to pay off the debts and interest and fund the high costs of maintenance. The defective original construction

Lighthouse, Crinan Canal
Peter Sandground

This attractive small, hexagonal, lighthouse, built in 1851 is located at the westernmost lock of the Crinan Canal and marks the start of the canal. It is painted white with a red band and has an external iron staircase. The building to the right is Seaview Cottage.

Locks, Crinan Canal
Peter Sandground

The Crinan Canal has fifteen locks and is crossed by seven bridges, six swing bridges and a retractable bridge. Stone for the fifteen locks was brought from Mull, the Isle of Arran and Morvern. From Ardrishaig, three locks raise the canal's four-mile long east reach to thirty-two feet above sea level. The 1,100-yard summit reach, between Cairnbaan and Dunardry, is sixty-four feet above sea level. The west reach between Dunardry and Crinan is eighteen feet above sea level. The canal is ten feet deep and has essentially no height limit. The retractable bridge at Lock 11 replaced the original swing bridge in 1900. It is operated by a rotating handle and a cogged wheel which causes the bridge deck to roll forwards and backwards on rails and comes to rest across the lock chamber. The canal has towpaths on both sides from Ardrishaig to Crinan Bridge and until 1959 horses assisted unpowered craft.

Rhubadach Cottage and Rolling Bridge, Crinan Canal
Peter Sandground

The lock-keeper's cottage at Dunardry Basin is being restored as a holiday property by Scottish Canals.

Crinan Canal Festival
Peter Sandground

The Mid-Argyll Pipe Band play on board 'VIC 32', the only coal-fired Puffer left in working operation, as she enters the canal basin to launch the Crinan Canal Classic Boat Festival in 2010. More than sixty classic sailing and motor-boats participated in races during the festival.

of the canal and its design for the age of sail, not steam, continued to handicap its successful operation. An Act of Parliament of 1848 transferred formal ownership of the Crinan Canal from the Barons of the Exchequer to the Commissioners of the Caledonian Canal.

We and our people drove through the little village to the Crinan Canal, where we entered a most magnificently decorated barge, drawn by three [four] horses, ridden by postilions in scarlet. We glided along very smoothly, and the view of the hills – the range of Cruachan – were very fine indeed; but the eleven locks we had to go through – (a very curious process, first passing several by rising, and then others by going down) – were tedious, and instead of the passage lasting one hour and a half, it lasted upwards of two hours and a half, therefore it was nearly eight o'clock before we reached Loch Crinan.

Queen Victoria's Journal for Wednesday 18 August 1847

Aided by Queen Victoria's visit in 1847, the tourist traffic on the canal reached over 44,000 passengers in 1857. The collapse of the Camloch embankment in February 1859 and subsequent closure of the canal for over a year caused another financial crisis. Special types of Puffer, or short steam-powered cargo boats, were developed to navigate from the River Clyde, through the canal and onwards to the rough seas of the West Coast. From 1881, the canal faced competition from the Oban railway. As the century progressed, various schemes came and went for enlarging the canal or constructing a new canal at Tarbert. Despite its inadequacies, a modest, but steady stream of income just about kept the canal going. Seventy-five percent of the revenue came from the north-ward passage of coal and general goods and the southward passage of slates, sand, granite, timber, kelp, livestock and farm produce.[20] As some trades died, for example herring fishing, others grew, such as the transport of whale oil from Harris. The new

fashion for leisure sailing off the West Coast saw a burgeoning passage of yachts and cruisers through the canal.

The route remained open during the First World War, but because Admiralty vessels paid no dues and passenger traffic was prohibited, revenues plummeted. The social, industrial, economic and military benefits of reconstructing the Crinan Canal as a modern ship canal were much discussed in the inter-war period, but always the costs of doing so were considered too high.[21] Undoubtedly, the canal had assumed a strategic importance in the economies of the Western Isles and the West Coast of the mainland. It was this strategic importance that secured a major investment of £100,000 in May 1930 by the new owners, the Ministry of Transport, to upgrade the existing canal by constructing new and accessible sea locks, an additional reservoir, and an increase of fifteen feet in depth at Ardrishaig Harbour. Losses on the canal were substantial in the post-war period, with new, larger, diesel Puffers

bypassing the Crinan route, but still its strategic social and economic importance to the West Coast saved it from the fate of the inland canals.

RENAISSANCE, 1980S–PRESENT DAY

Commercial use of the Crinan Canal declined in the 1960s and 1970s, but the canal has seen a revival in other uses through leisure and tourism. Extensive improvements to the banks between Bellanoch and Crinan were carried out in 1991 to reduce leakage. Although the canal itself carries little freight, the harbour at Ardrishaig has been developed to handle increasing quantities of timber. The Ardrishaig masterplan of 2009 sets out proposals for regeneration of the southern gateway to the canal. The canal corridor has formed a key element of the Dalriada Project, a programme for promoting understanding and promotion of Argyll's heritage and wildlife through interactive panels, podcasts and other materials and activities.[22]

Caledonian Canal

Caledonian Canal

D. Houghton / Scottish Viewpoint

Linking the lochs of the Great Glen, the Caledonian Canal provided a safe route for naval and merchant ships to avoid the treacherous Pentland Firth and Cape Wrath. Statesman engineer, Thomas Telford oversaw the mammoth undertaking from 1804. Eventually completed in 1822, the Caledonian Canal was rightly regarded then, as now, as a triumph of civil engineering.

About the Middle of the Neck of Land, that divides the Lakes Oick and Lochy, (which is but one Mile) not far from the Center of the Opening, there descends from the Hills, on the South-Side, a Burne or Rivulet, which, as it falls upon the Plain, divides into two Streams, without any visible Ridge to part them. And one of them runs through the Lakes Oick and Ness into the East-Sea, and the other takes the quite contrary Course, and passes through Loch Lochy, into the Western Ocean. This, and the short Space of Land above mentioned, have given Birth to several Projects for making a navigable Communication across the Island; not only to divide, effectually, the Highlands by the Middle, but to save the tedious, costly and hazardous Voyages through St. George's Channel, or otherwise round by the Isles of Orkney.

Edward Burt, *Letters from A Gentleman in the North of Scotland to His Friend in London*, 1737[1]

The Caledonian Canal is a ship canal, built by the government to connect the Beauly Firth and Inverness on the east coast to Loch Linnhe and Corpach on the west coast via the chain of lochs of the Great Glen: Lochs Dochfour, Ness, Oich and Lochy. The lochs both feed and connect the manmade sections of canal. At over seventeen feet deep, fifty feet wide at the bottom, 110 feet wide at the surface, and some sixty miles in total length, the Caledonian Canal is by far the largest, grandest and most expensive product of Scotland's canal mania. Two-thirds of the length of the route is comprised of the natural lochs. These are linked by four sections of manmade canal totalling twenty-two miles in length: Inverness (Clachnaharry) to Lochs Dochfour and Ness; Fort Augustus to Loch Oich; Loch Oich to Loch Lochy; and Loch Lochy to Corpach. The water levels were raised and channels dredged in Lochs Dochfour and Oich, but Lochs Ness and Lochy were already deep enough for navigation by ocean-going vessels. Apart from the regulating locks, which controlled the water levels at the entrances and exits of the natural lochs, the twenty-eight (later

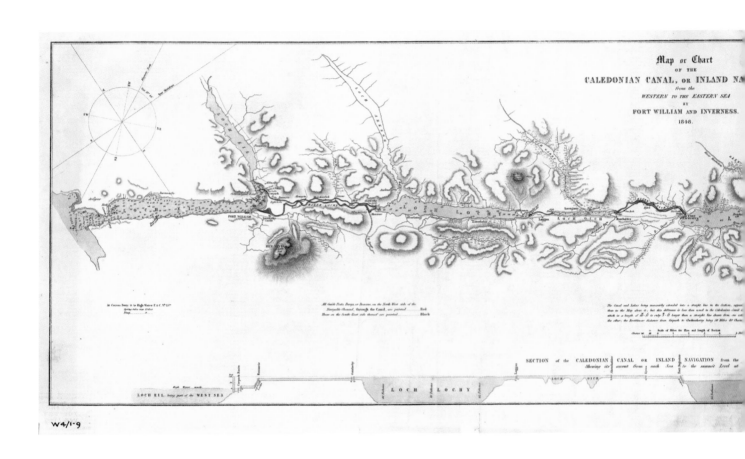

Map or Chart
OF THE
CALEDONIAN CANAL, OR INLAND NA
from the
WESTERN TO THE EASTERN SEA
BY
FORT WILLIAM AND INVERNESS.
1848.

twenty-nine) masonry locks were sited in clusters and designed at 170 feet in length and forty feet in width to accommodate the medium-sized thirty-two-gun frigates of the Royal Navy of the time.

PLANNING THE CANAL, EARLY EIGHTEENTH CENTURY TO 1803

Famously, the prediction that 'One day ships will sail round the back of Tomnahurich Hill' (the distinctive rounded hill on the outskirts of Inverness) is attributed to Coinneach Odhar Fiosaiche, or the Brahan Seer, in the mid seventeenth-century.[2] As Edward Burt indicated in his *Letters from A Gentleman in the North of Scotland to His Friend in London* of 1737, a number of proposals for a canal were drawn up in the early eighteenth century. However,

it was 1773 before James Watt devised a serious Fort William to Inverness scheme for consideration by the Lords Commissioners of Police.[3] John Rennie made a further survey in 1793. In view of the continuing catastrophic social and economic state of the Highlands in the aftermath of the 1745 Jacobite Rising, the high rate of emigration caused by the clearances and the destitution following the crop failures of 1799 and 1800, the government eventually commissioned a survey and report on the situation from Thomas Telford in 1802.[4]

Telford's report made practical recommendations for unprecedented government-funded infrastructure projects that would both create local employment to prevent emigration and open up wider trading opportunities through new roads,

Map or Chart of the Caledonian Canal, 1848
Scottish Canals

The Caledonian Canal finally opened in 1822, having taken twelve years longer to complete than anticipated. It cost £910,000 and over 3,000 local people had been employed in its construction. In an effort to save costs the draught had been reduced from twenty feet to fifteen feet. Before long, defects in some of the materials used became apparent, and part of Corpach double lock collapsed in 1843. This led to a decision to close the canal to allow repairs to be carried out, and the depth was increased to eighteen feet at the same time. The work was designed by Telford's associate James Walker, and completed by 1847.

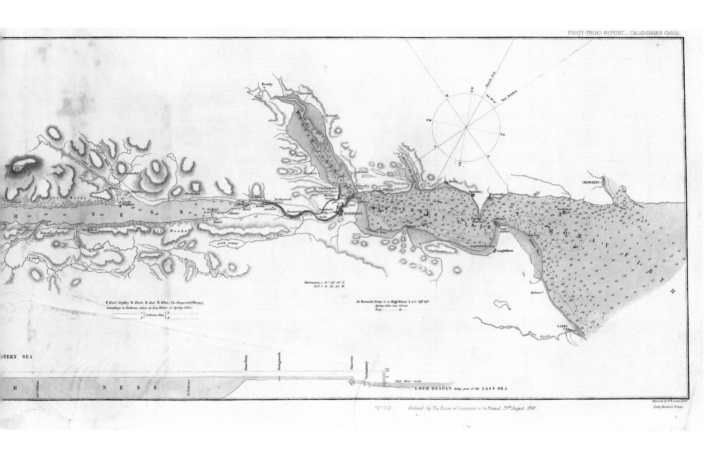

bridges, harbours and the revived idea of a canal. Against the backdrop of increasing hostilities with France, the canal project also took on a strategic importance as a safe route connecting the east to the west coast. Supported by the Highland Society of Scotland, the British Fisheries Society and numerous local landowners, the government accepted Telford's recommendations and initial estimate of £350,000 for a seven-year project. In 1803, 'An Act for granting to his Majesty the Sum of £20,000, towards defraying the Expense of making an Inland Navigation from the western to the eastern Sea, by Inverness and Fort William; and for taking the necessary steps towards executing the same', enabled the formation in London of the Board of Commissioners for the Caledonian Canal

and the start of an enormous project that was to take nineteen years to open in an incomplete state and at an eventual cost of over £900,000.[5]

BUILDING THE CANAL, 1804–47

Thomas Telford was appointed chief engineer on a salary of three guineas a day plus expenses, and started work on a detailed survey with William Jessop, his former mentor and a pupil of John Smeaton. Jessop's role in the construction of the canal has often been underplayed, not least by Telford himself in his autobiography, but Jessop was the older man and significantly more experienced in canal-building, and the commissioners clearly regarded him as their chief consulting engineer.[6] Telford sought Jessop's advice on numerous

Portrait of Thomas Telford by Sir Henry Raeburn, about 1803
National Museums, Liverpool

Thomas Telford (1757–1834) was a Scottish civil engineer, architect and stonemason, and a noted road, bridge and canal builder. After establishing himself as an engineer of road and canal projects in Shropshire, he designed numerous infrastructure projects in his native Scotland, as well as harbours and tunnels. Such was his reputation as a prolific designer of highways and related bridges, he was dubbed 'the Colossus of Roads'.

occasions, and the two men appear to have shared their responsibilities amicably. Murdoch Downie carried out a hydrographic survey of the lochs at the same time. Construction began in 1804 on the basins at both ends of the canal with two resident superintendent engineers (Matthew Davidson, known as 'the Walking Library', based in Inverness, and John Telford, no relation of Thomas, in Fort William) overseeing the foremen, the principal masonry contractor, John Simpson of Shrewsbury, and teams of other contractors working on small tendered lots of cutting, puddling and embankment work.[7] Many of Telford's senior team had previously worked with him and William Jessop on the construction of the extraordinary Pontcysyllte Aqueduct on the Llangollen Canal in North Wales.[8]

Not all the necessary land had been purchased before the work began, so construction took place simultaneously in several places along the route where the canal commissioners had taken ownership.[9] The intention was to supply materials to the middle sections by means of the completed ends of the canal. The scale of the project was indeed daunting, as James Hogg, the poet and novelist known as the Ettrick Shepherd, reported from Corpach in 1804:

...while observing how carelessly the labourers were dabbing with their picks and spades, and how apt they were to look around them at every thing which was to be seen; while others were winding slowly out with each a little gravel in a wheelbarrow, – I say, while contemplating the exertions of these men, and wishing to anticipate in my mind the important aera when they should join Lochiel to the Moray Firth, at above fifty miles distance, I could not help viewing it as a hopeless job: my head grew somewhat dizzy, and I felt the same sort of quandary that I used to do formerly when thinking of eternity.[10]

While much of the work was done by hand or horsepower, new Boulton & Watt steam engines drove both pumps for removing water from the construction sites and the pioneering purpose-built bucket-dredgers employed for clearing the navigation channels through the lochs.

A number of the contractors had worked with Telford on the Ellesmere Canal, and also tendered for Telford's road and bridge projects in the Highlands. Such was the size of the project and the lack of facilities on site that temporary accommodation huts, timber yards, stables and workshops were built at Corpach and Clachnaharry, and oatmeal and milk supplied to workers at cost price.[11] Numbers of workers varied from year to year and from season to season (depending on other seasonal activities, such as herring fishing and potato planting/harvesting), but on average about 1,000 were employed at any one time, divided fairly evenly between the eastern and western districts of the project. The manual labour was hard, physical, and occasionally dangerous, requiring skill and high levels of fitness and stamina. Recruitment of suitable workers was a continual problem throughout the project. At first many of the navvies were recruited locally, as originally intended, but later

On the Caledonian Canal at Muirtown by James Valentine
Private Collection

Taken in about 1880, this atmospheric view of the lowest of the four locks at Muirtown in Inverness demonstrates the scale of the engineering and the significant manpower required to operate the capstans of the lock-gates. The 180-foot-long by forty-foot-wide locks on the Caledonian Canal, designed to accommodate Royal Navy frigates, were the largest in the world at the time of construction. Contractors Simpson & Cargill built the Muirtown Locks in 1808–13. They raise the canal some twenty-three feet above the Muirtown Basin.

controversy raged over the supposed high numbers of incomers employed on the scheme.[12] Telford responded by producing figures to demonstrate the low proportion of incomers in the workforce. Other critics doubted the effect of the canal project on reducing emigration from the Highlands. Writing in 1887, the Inverness architect Alexander Ross, believed that the canal had produced the opposite effect, increasing emigration by providing local workers with the means, skills and education to escape from the squalor.[13] However, Ross noted the beneficial effects of agricultural improvement along the route of the canal for those who survived the depopulation.

In order to save construction costs, the non-regulating locks were grouped, notably at Banavie where the exceptional flight of eight consecutive locks, named 'Neptune's Staircase' by the workmen, raised the level of the canal sixty-two feet by the end of 1819.[14] Stone for the locks was quarried from local quarries and from parts of the canal channel itself. Local timber was used for utilitarian

purposes, such as making wheelbarrows and temporary coffer dams, but for important structural elements, such as the lock-gates, high-quality American pitch-pine was framed in cast iron. As the canal was intended for sea-going sailing ships, Telford proposed cast-iron swing-bridges to allow a clear passage for masts. However, steam-powered ships had gained such a foothold by 1813 that Telford abandoned the original plans for a towpath along Loch Oich, which would have allowed sailing ships to be towed when there were strong contrary winds. Progress was slow for a number of reasons: the government funding of £50,000 was granted on an annual basis, limiting how much work could be done in a year; the Napoleonic Wars and trade blockades had a significant inflationary effect on wages and materials from 1806, reducing the spending power of the annual grant; a major land dispute broke out between the canal commissioners and Colonel Alexander Ronaldson MacDonnell of Clanronald and Glengarry; and a number of unexpected engineering problems presented themselves as the work got underway. Chief among the numerous challenges was the general need

Tomnahurich Swing Bridge View of Tail End and Deck under Construction, Caledonian Canal ←
RCAHMS

This view from the archives of Sir William Arrol & Co. shows the Tomnahurich swing bridge under construction in 1938. It was jointly designed by the engineers Crouch & Hogg and T. Shirley Hawkins to cater for the increase in vehicle traffic over the canal.

Corpach and Lighthouse, Caledonian Canal →↓
Nick Haynes

Corpach was the southern centre for construction of the canal, serving as a base for the workshops, housing workers and horses, and handling the enormous quantities of materials. A small stone stable and masons' store survives from 1808. The original four-storey lock-keeper's house was replaced by the current whitewashed house and office in about 1913. The Corpach navigation light marks the southern entrance to the Caledonian Canal from Loch Linnhe.

Former Engine House, Fort Augustus Locks, Caledonian Canal ↙
RCAHMS

Reputedly an eighteenth-century gunpowder store associated with the fort, this small building was converted for use as the engine house to pump out the water during the construction of the Fort Augustus locks. According to the Report of the Commissioners for the Caledonian Canal of 1818, the engine house and engine cost £1,279.

Aerial View of Fort Augustus Locks, Caledonian Canal
RCAHMS

Aerial View of Neptune's Staircase, Caledonian Canal →
RCAHMS

Neptune's Staircase and Telford House, Banavie, Caledonian Canal
Nick Haynes

The flight of eight locks at Banavie, known as 'Neptune's Staircase' is undoubtedly the most spectacular of the lock groupings on the Caledonian Canal. Contractors Simpson & Wilson built the locks between 1808 and 1811 under the supervision of the resident engineer, Alexander Easton. Twelve lock-keepers were required to operate the flight. All the gates are now mechanised and the journey through takes about an hour and a half. The celebrated poet and friend of Telford, Robert Southey, wrote an 'inscription' in praise of the staircase in 1829:

Where these capacious basins, by the laws
Of the subjacent element receive
The ship, descending or upraised, eight times,
From stage to stage with unfelt agency
Translated; fitliest may the marble here
Record the Architect's immortal name.
Telford it was, by whose presiding mind
The whole great work was plann'd and perfected;

Robert Southey, *At Banavie*, 1829

Fort Augustus Locks, Caledonian Canal ↗
Peter Sandground

Went before breakfast to look at the locks, five together, of which three are finished, the fourth about half-built, the fifth not quite excavated. Such an extent of masonry, upon such a scale, I had never before beheld, each of these Locks being 180 feet in length. It was a most impressive and rememberable scene. Men, horses, and machines at work; digging, walling and puddling going on, men wheeling barrows, horses drawing stones along the railways. The great steam engine was at rest, having done its work.

Robert Southey, *Journal of a Tour in Scotland*, 16 September 1820

Locks at Muirtown, Caledonian Canal →
Nick Haynes

The Muirtown lock-gates are now mechanised, but the passage through all four locks still takes about an hour to complete.

Telford House, Gairlochy, Caledonian Canal
Peter Sandground

Thomas Telford designed this as a bridge- and
lock-keepers' house about 1811. It was used initially
as accommodation for the construction workers
on Gairlochy Lock and Bridge, and Telford himself
stayed there during his supervisory visits. The central
bowed bay allowed views up and down the canal
to approaching boats. Similar houses were built at
Banavie.

to protect the works from water ingress during
construction, the excavation of the Corpach Basin
and the Laggan Cutting from solid rock, local
ground conditions and the building of the huge
masonry lock-pits. Jessop retired due to ill health
in 1812. John Telford died in 1807 and Matthew
Davidson died in 1819, to be replaced respectively
by Alexander Easton and James Davidson.

As the works dragged on and the costs spiralled,
the political appetite in London for continued
government funding dwindled. In spite of the
opening of the eastern section from Inverness to
Loch Ness in May 1818, the following year there
were increasing calls for the whole scheme to be
abandoned. The project remained on a knife-edge.
Finally, the Loch Ness steam yacht undertook the
first end-to-end thirteen-hour passage of the canal

between 23 and 24 October 1822, and was greeted
by crowds of enthusiastic well-wishers, bands and
celebratory cannon-fire along the route.[15]

However, with the water depth at only twelve feet
instead of the planned twenty feet, the canal
remained far from complete.[16] The advances in
steam power also endangered the profitability of
the canal, as the treacherous Pentland Firth could
now be more easily navigated by steamboat and
without canal dues. Strategic benefits were limited
too, now that the wars with France were at an end.
The canal remained in a persistent state of financial
distress throughout the second quarter of the nineteenth century, with the canal dues falling far short
of the substantial maintenance costs, let alone the
sums required for completion.

A number of defects in the construction of the

Moy Turn-Bridge and House, Caledonian Canal
Peter Sandground

The forty-foot span of the turn-bridge at Moy was constructed in 1820 to a pattern developed from the bridges of Jessop's West India Docks in London. It is the only original cast-iron bridge surviving over the canal and is still hand-operated. Iron was brought from the Plas Kynaston foundry of William Hazeline, Telford's contractor for the Pontcysyllte Aqueduct on the Llangollen Canal. The bridge swings in two parts, which requires users to row across the canal to open and close the bridge. The former bridge-keeper's cottage stands at the southern end of the bridge.

Lock-gate on the Caledonian Canal with Meall an t-Slamain in the Background
Nick Haynes

Torcastle Aqueduct, Caledonian Canal
Nick Haynes

This substantial aqueduct, comprising two 240-foot-long tunnels over Allt Sheangain and a further pedestrian tunnel, was one of five constructed by the contractors Simpson & Wilson on the Banavie to Achnacarry stretch of the canal before 1808.

locks soon became apparent. These were laid at the door of one of the contractors, who was thought to have hidden substandard work from Telford's watchful eye.[17] By the late 1830s there were serious concerns about the threat to life and property from the poor condition of the canal, in spite of the resident engineer George May's best efforts to avert disasters. After much procrastination and controversy, the government authorised a scheme by the engineers James Walker and Alfred Burges to thoroughly repair and complete the canal to a depth of seventeen feet in 1843.[18] It reopened in May 1847.[19] Amongst new works, the scheme added a new lock at Gairlochy to deal with the threat of flooding at Loch Lochy, and navigational aids and lighting at the entrances to the canal. Prince Albert took in the newly refurbished canal as part of a successful visit to Dochfour and Inverness in September 1847.[20] Four new steam tugs were provided to encourage use of the canal by sailing ships, which had always struggled with contrary winds through the lochs.

From 1848 the Commissioners of the Caledonian Canal also took on responsibility for the Crinan Canal, but still managed the two enterprises separately. Even though the works of the 1840s had been executed to a high quality, there were still areas of weakness, notably in the construction of the old locks fitted with cast-iron gates. Between 1861 and 1875 the revenues just about exceeded expenditure in most years, and after that were more volatile, with relatively minor losses in some years. By 1888 the cast-iron gates were in a fragile condition and a new programme of replacement timber gates was begun, which was finally completed in 1906. The opening of the West Highland Railway's branch to Banavie in 1895 and the Invergarry and Fort Augustus Railway in 1903 provided a mild stimulus to passenger and goods trade respectively.

Although the canal was busy during the First World War, much of the traffic was on government service and could not be charged. From 1919, the year in which responsibility transferred to the Ministry of Transport, expenditure was always in

Bona Lighthouse, Caledonian Canal
Peter Sandground

The octagonal Bona Lighthouse was designed by Telford in about 1815 to mark the entrance to Loch Dochfour from the northern end of Loch Ness. Scottish Canals undertook a major repair and refurbishment of the building in 2014 for its new use as a holiday cottage.

multiples of the revenue. In spite of raising charges, the ministry found it impossible to balance the books in the face of the high maintenance and repair costs and competition from the railways and motorbuses. The heavily increased expenditure in the 1930s can be attributed to the ministry's investment in upgrading the road bridges for the new age of motor transport. Continuing problems with the walls of the lock and decay of the timber lock-gates, combined with general neglect after the Second World War, led to a series of collapses, most seriously at Corpach in 1964, but also at Laggan and Kytra.[21] By this time most of the canal traffic comprised fishing vessels.

The 1958 Bowes Committee of Inquiry into Inland Waterways had concluded that 'We see no prospect that either of them [the two Highland canals] will become a viable, commercial undertaking, but they play an important part in the social and economic life of large areas in the west and north of the country, and if long-term policies in relation to those areas attain their aims, the waterways may become more valuable as transport media.'[22] Holding repairs were made to keep the canal operational, and there was investment in new mechanised lock-gates at a cost of £195,000 between 1958 and 1968.[23]

MV Kanutta on the Caledonian Canal
Peter Sandground

Scottish Government grants of £255,000 heralded the return of freight transportation along the Caledonian Canal, which will benefit the environment by removing over 15,000 lorry trips from the road network. The successful maiden voyage through the canal was made by MV Kanutta.

RENAISSANCE, 1976–PRESENT DAY

Increasing leisure and tourist activity followed the 150th anniversary of the canal in 1972, with cruise holidays becoming popular. However, the canal's poor condition had become a matter of considerable concern by the time of a report to the Department of the Environment by Peter Faenkel & Partners on all the British Waterways Board canals in 1975.[24] Another collapse of the locks at Laggan finally convinced the government to authorise their repair and to begin a programme to replace all the lock-gates. Many of the road bridges were repaired and renovated in 1980–1 and further substantial repairs were undertaken to many of the locks throughout the 1980s. A radar survey of all the locks in 1995 revealed a worrying level of unseen decay that launched a Scottish Government-funded £20m comprehensive lock stabilisation programme along the entire length of the canal between 1996 and 2006.[25] The Great Glen Way Initiative in 2007–8 saw the installation of forty-nine information and interpretation panels along the Caledonian Canal.[26] Development continues of the Seaport Marina at Muirtown Basin, Inverness and other berthing facilities along the route.[27]

Union Canal

Ashley Terrace Boathouse at Lockhart Bridge in Edinburgh is the base for the Edinburgh Canal Society, a charitable canal society founded in 1985. The society's boathouse was dismantled and rebuilt in modified form in 1987 and is one of the most distinctive buildings on the Lowland canals. In 2009, the society was involved in setting up the Edinburgh Canal Festival, which is now an annual event.

The advantages attending this great undertaking are said to be highly important. It will open an inland navigation between Scotland and the west of England, and the whole of Ireland: Coach passengers, parcels, and land-carriage of goods betwixt Edinburgh and Glasgow, amount to about L.70,000 yearly; this sum, it is said, the Union Canal will lessen one-third. Coal will be only two-thirds of its present price to the inhabitants of Edinburgh. Coal and lime will form its principal trade, as the line through which it passes is said to contain inexhaustible quantities, besides freestone and ironstone. It has been calculated that the Union Canal will pay 20 per cent on the outlay, after deducting all expences.

The Stranger's Guide to Edinburgh, 1817[1]

The full name of the Edinburgh and Glasgow Union Canal is misleading, as in fact the thirty-one-mile canal runs from the capital only as far as Falkirk, from which point the Forth and Clyde Canal forms the connection to Glasgow.[2] Like the Monkland Canal, it was a shallow (five feet deep) 'level line' or contour canal, following the meanderings of the 240-foot-contour to avoid the expensive construction and time delays of locks. It is thirty-seven feet wide at the surface and twenty feet wide at the bottom.[3] Of all the surviving canals, the Union Canal has some of the most dramatic engineering structures, represented in the series of aqueducts that keep its path level over roads and rivers, the 690-yard long tunnel skirting the Callendar Estate at Falkirk, and the many road bridges that cross it. The canal underwent a substantial restoration programme in the late 1990s, culminating in the re-establishment of a link to the Forth and Clyde Canal via the spectacular Falkirk Wheel in 2002.

PLANNING THE CANAL, 1791–1817

The Union Canal has other similarities with the earlier Monkland Canal. It owes its existence to a late eighteenth-century desire to stimulate competition and lessen the price of coal, in this case for Edinburgh and Leith. Coal brought from Alloa, Fife

and Newcastle via the River Forth was subject to duty, and the poor road network and inefficient cartage from Midlothian also added to the costs of the city's fuel. Unlike the Monkland Canal, which began on site within months of its conception, the planning of the Union Canal soon became bogged down in arguments between the various vested interests in the scheme, and took the best part of two decades to get off the drawing board.

'Country-gentlemen of great respectability', including Colonel George Dalrymple and Thomas Elder of Forneth, first proposed a canal connecting Leith to the Broomielaw quays in Glasgow via the coalfields of Lanarkshire south of Shotts in 1791.[4] The scheme made further progress in 1793, when John Ainslie and Robert Whitworth Junior, engineers, made a survey of four possible routes for the subscribers' committee, and John Grieve and James Taylor, mineral surveyors, examined the extent of coal, ironstone and other minerals adjacent to the lines.[5] In September 1797 the

engineer John Rennie reported to the committee of subscribers on the four routes and added his own suggested northern route from Leith via Linlithgow and Falkirk to Drumpellier on the Monkland Canal.[6] Rennie's route required fewer locks, but it also passed further away from the coalfields than the Ainslie/Whitworth proposals. With economic uncertainty and public controversy surrounding the routes, the outbreak of war with France in 1803 saw the project shelved.

It was 1813 before a new scheme emerged. The then resident engineer of the Forth and Clyde Canal, Hugh Baird, was responsible for planning the new route from Lothian Road in Edinburgh to a junction at lock sixteen of the Forth and Clyde just south of Camelon, near Falkirk.[7] Baird estimated his thirty-one-and-a-half mile scheme at about half the cost of Rennie's previous sixty-four mile proposal, largely because it avoided creating an expensive series of locks from Leith and a long cross-country route to Drumpellier. Almost every aspect of

Avon and Slateford Aqueducts, Union Canal ←↓
Peter Sandground | RCAHMS

A guidebook, published in 1823, described the attractions of the journey from east to west, especially the three major aqueducts. The first, at Slateford, spanned the Water of Leith in eight 'lofty' arches; the second spanned the River Almond at Lin's Mill in five arches; and the grandest of the three, the twelve-arched Avon Aqueduct at Linlithgow.

Prince Charlie Aqueduct, Union Canal
RCAHMS

This wide, single-spanned concrete aqueduct, built in 1937, carries the Union Canal across Slateford Road in Edinburgh. It replaced the original stone-built aqueduct, designed about 1821 by Hugh Baird.

the project remained controversial, particularly amongst supporters of a terminus in Leith and those who felt that the route would perpetuate the monopoly of the Forth and Clyde Canal Company.[8] The canal subscribers brought in the eminent engineer Thomas Telford to back the scheme by Baird, whilst the Edinburgh Town Council commissioned Robert Stevenson to develop another alternative route.[9] As a further enticement, the subscribers offered a free, and much-needed, water supply to the city via the canal.

BUILDING THE CANAL, 1818–24

After much wrangling, 'an Act for making and maintaining a navigable Canal from the Lothian Road, near the city of Edinburgh, to join the Forth and Clyde Navigation near Falkirk, in the county of Stirling' was finally granted royal assent on 27 June 1817.[10] The Act enabled the incorporation of the Edinburgh and Glasgow Union Canal Company with capital of £245,000, comprising shares of

£50 each.[11] Although Hugh Baird was appointed as the project engineer on a salary of £500 per annum, Thomas Telford remained heavily involved, providing amongst other things estimates for the reservoirs and feeders, divisions of the work into lots for contractors, specifications for cutting of the canal, embanking, lining, puddling, fencing, and road bridges and aqueducts, and advice on minor deviations of the route.[12]

The route needed only eleven locks, which were grouped in a single spectacular flight at Summerford near the junction with the Forth and Clyde Canal, but a large number of feeders, drains, cuttings, embankments, aqueducts and bridges were required to maintain the level line. Baird, with advice from Telford, designed three major stone aqueducts with cast-iron troughs to cross the Water of Leith at Slateford (eight arches, seventy-five feet high, 500 feet long), the River Almond at Lin's Mill (five arches, seventy-five feet high, 420 feet long) and the River Avon, west of Linlithgow

(twelve arches, eighty-five feet high, 810 feet long).
A source of considerable annoyance and expense
to the canal company was the stipulation of the
1817 Act to avoid the policies of Callendar House
on the outskirts of Falkirk which was owned by a
successful businessman and entrepreneur, William
Forbes. This required the construction of a 690-yard
hand-hewn tunnel through Prospect Hill to the west
of the estate.

In spite of difficulties with some of the contractors and labourers, construction progress was
swift. Work began at the basin in Fountainbridge,
Edinburgh, on 4 March 1818. The Revd David
Dickson read an 'impressive prayer' and the president of the canal company, Robert Downie of Appin,
cut the first turf.[13] A year later, nearly fourteen
miles had been excavated, and on 16 January 1821
the first boat crossed the Avon Aqueduct in front
of cheering crowds.[14] By the beginning of 1822
residents of Linlithgow and Stirlingshire were
reporting the extraordinary sight of lines of blazing
torches in the countryside, as work on the canal
continued through the night.[15] The tunnel remained
the last major obstacle to completion of the route.
On 9 March 1822 the entire length of the canal was
filled with water, and the two passenger boats,

General View Showing Infilling at Hopetoun Basin, Union Canal ←
RCAHMS

North British Rubber Company, Union Canal ↙
RCAHMS

In 1856, a wealthy American, Henry Lee Norris, established the North British Rubber Company in the buildings of the former Castle Silk Mills beside the Union Canal. The company introduced the manufacture of rubber goods into Scotland and was the industry leader in the development of rubber manufacture. The Castle Mills headquarters covered over five acres of land and in the 1890s the factory employed around 1,600 people. The company made all kinds of rubber goods including waterproof clothing and footwear, surgical, household and mechanical apparatus, bicycle tyres and trench boots used by soldiers during the First World War. In 1963 it was the largest manufacturing concern in the east of Scotland. It moved to Newbridge in the late 1960s, and the Castle Mills were demolished.

Lochrin Basin and Wooden Drawbridge, Union Canal ↗→
RCAHMS

The original terminus of the canal was at Port Hopetoun, a large basin situated next to Lothian Road. Another basin, Port Hamilton was built later as traffic increased. As well as passengers there was an important passage into the city of coal, grain and building materials, although only waste was exported from the city via the canal. However, as trade declined, the area degenerated and Port Hopetoun and Port Hamilton were closed in 1922. A new terminus was created on the south side of Fountainbridge at Lochrin Basin, on an offshoot of the main canal, which served Haig's Distillery.

Warehouse at Port Hopetoun, Union Canal
RCAHMS

This unusual three-storeyed warehouse, with huge storeyed timber 'wings' that extended from each end wall, was one of the most remarkable canal buildings in Scotland. It stood at the quayside at Port Hopetoun, the eastern terminal basin of the canal at Lothian Road, and was built to cope with the considerable passenger traffic into the port in the mid-nineteenth century. The building was demolished when the basin was abandoned in 1922. At the height of the canal trade in the mid-nineteenth century, goods traffic into Port Hopetoun grew rapidly, stretching the limited facilities of the port. New buildings were constructed to cope with the increased traffic, including this large building, which was constructed for the 'luggage-boat companies' on the square where passengers landed. Other new buildings included offices, warehouses and dwelling houses.

Francis M. Chrystal was the second son of the former Professor of Mathematics at the University of Edinburgh. He attended George Watson's College, Edinburgh and was one of the original members of the Old Edinburgh Club, contributing views of historic buildings and closes to the club's volumes. He also produced many startling images of the Union Canal including these two group portraits. He died in 1944.

'Flora McIvor' and 'Die Vernon', were towed into the Port Hopetoun Basin at Fountainbridge.[16] The first cargo of Denny flagstones to travel the whole length of the canal arrived at Port Hopetoun on 10 May.[17] By 1824, when much of the finishing off had been completed, some £600,000 had been spent on the project – almost two-and-a-half times the initial estimate.[18]

DECLINE AND CLOSURE, 1842–1965

The Union Canal had several debt repayment crises and a short period of profitable operation before the opening of the Edinburgh and Glasgow Railway in February 1842 and the Caledonian's rival Edinburgh to Glasgow service in February 1848. With Edinburgh to Glasgow journeys of up to fourteen hours (including a walk or a coach from Port Maxwell to Port Downie on the Forth and Clyde Canal), the Union Canal was unable to compete with the speed and convenience of the two-hour journey by rail from city centre to city centre. Unsurprisingly, the Union Canal's passenger traffic plummeted. Relatively little goods trade came out of Edinburgh, but substantial quantities of timber, stone, brick, slate, lime, sand and coal were brought in.[19] The goods traffic had a more prolonged decline, but was also adversely affected by the railway's ability to provide branch lines and sidings directly into factories and works, avoiding the need to transfer materials and goods between canal boats and other forms of transport for distribution and delivery.

Having cut fares and dues in an attempt to compete with the railways, the canal company threw in the towel in 1849, selling its assets to the Edinburgh and Glasgow Railway Company.[20] The railway company took on the obligations to keep the canal in good working order, and these were subsequently transferred to the North British Railway Company on its amalgamation with the Edinburgh and Glasgow Railway Company in 1865. In spite of efforts to encourage the transport of coal, revenues dwindled to £5,209 in 1870 and just £3,267 in 1900.[21] The Port Hamilton and Port Hopetoun Basins were abandoned and sold in 1921 and a new

Leamington Lift Bridge, Union Canal
Peter Sandground | RCAHMS

This is a distinctive and unusual early twentieth-century lifting bridge. It has a rivetted steel framework and a short lifting span. The control cabin is incorporated within the framework, and when the bridge is lifted to allow boats to pass through, pedestrians can still cross by the lattice girder footbridge. The Leamington Bridge was originally at Fountainbridge and replaced a wooden drawbridge at the time of the closure of the city basins in 1922. The current location is close to the present end of the canal.

Soliton Wave, Union Canal
Peter Sandground

The Soliton Wave was recreated on the Union Canal, during filming for BBC TV series 'Coast'. In maths and physics a soliton is a self-reinforcing solitary wave (a wave packet or pulse) that maintains its shape while it propagates at a constant velocity. The great scientist, engineer and naval architect, John Scott Russell, first described the phenomenon in 1834 after witnessing a wave rolling forward from the front of a canal boat when the vessel stopped suddenly at Hermiston on the Union Canal.

eastern terminus established at Lochrin Basin. However, commercial traffic ceased completely in 1933, after which the great flight of locks at Summerford and the Port Downie Basin were filled in.[22] The canal continued in use for a small number of pleasure craft and as a water supply to various industrial enterprises in Edinburgh, Linlithgow and Falkirk. The City and Royal Burgh of Edinburgh Development Plan of 1953 proposed formal closure of the Union Canal, which further prompted by safety concerns and the potential development of Wester Hailes for housing came about in August 1965. The canal quickly clogged with weeds and rubbish, and when the Wester Hailes development proceeded, a one-mile section of the canal was filled in. The construction of the M8 and the Edinburgh City Bypass added major impediments to the route of the canal.

RENAISSANCE, 1970–PRESENT DAY
As with the Forth and Clyde Canal, amenity body interest in reviving the Union Canal grew throughout the 1970s and 1980s, eventually prompting interest at official level. Local residents began clearing the towpath at Linlithgow in 1970, and the Linlithgow Union Canal Society was founded there in 1975. A Joint Working Party established in 1971 became the Union Canal Development Group in 1975, publishing a report on the recreation and amenity possibilities of the canal in 1977. The floating restaurant 'Pride of the Union', reintroduced large boats to the canal in 1974.[23] The Edinburgh Canal Society formed in 1986.

The Millennium Link project of 1999–2002, outlined in the chapter on the Forth and Clyde Canal, had a similarly radical effect on the Union Canal. Seven new road bridges and three foot-bridges along with the reinstated canal at Wester Hailes were opened on 25 August 2001.

The great symbol of Scotland's Millennium canal renaissance is The Falkirk Wheel, a rotating lift for eight or more boats, built by Butterley Engineering in 2001 from designs by Morrison-Bachy-Soletanche contractors with RMJM architects,

Arup Consultants, Butterley Engineering, Tony Gee & Partners and Bennett Associates (based on an initial concept by Nicoll Russell Studios and engineers Babtie Group).[24] From an early stage in the design of the Millennium Link project it was decided that twenty-first-century engineering should replace the flight of eleven locks at Tamfourhill, which before their destruction in 1933 had lowered the Union Canal eighty-two feet to the level of the Forth and Clyde Canal. The wheel stands at Roughcastle on a site west of the old locks. It required the construction of a new three-quarters-of-a-mile section of canal, two upper locks, a 482-foot-long tunnel beneath the Antonine Wall and Edinburgh to Glasgow railway, a 360-foot-long aqueduct, upper and lower basins, and a lower lock and footbridge. Her Majesty The Queen opened the new link on 24 May 2002.

The revived canal has stimulated increased activity on the canal and a number of new and potential developments around it, including the major Edinburgh Quay development by Miller Developments and British Waterways of 2002–3, the marina and housing at Ratho, the evolving former Fountain Brewery site and the proposed marina at Tamfourhill. At the eastern end of the canal, the 2011 Edinburgh Union Canal Strategy guides development.

Wester Hailes, Union Canal
Peter Sandground

The Union Canal was officially closed in 1965 and subsequently a section of the canal was filled-in to allow for new housing at Wester Hailes. In 1994 British Waterways proposed the restoration of the Union and Forth and Clyde Canals with fully navigable waterways which would link up the two coasts. To do this, the infilled section of canal was reinstated in what was Scotland's most expensive Millennium project.

Leamington Wharf, Union Canal
Peter Sandground

Leamington Wharf in Edinburgh, is part of the Living on Water Initiative being run by Scottish Canals to bring new vibrancy to Scotland's canals by encouraging more people to live and work on the water. It is part of an overall strategy to deliver sustainable development and improvements to Scotland's canals and towpaths.

Ten Year Celebration, Union Canal
Peter Sandground

The Union Canal was one of the last canals ever built in Britain. It was almost immediately overshadowed by the faster rail network in 1849. By 1965 the canal was closed, and became a stagnant ditch, receiving minimal maintenance to prevent leaks. Blocked by roads and housing development in the late twentieth century the canal almost disappeared. Due to the efforts of many enthusiasts, community campaigning and the foresight shown by bodies such as Scottish Canals the Union Canal has reopened. The canal now forms a unique wildlife corridor connecting the heart of Edinburgh with the rural countryside and linking with the Forth and Clyde Canal via The Falkirk Wheel. The successful Millennium lottery bid that made the project possible has at its heart the notion that a redeveloped canal has the potential to regenerate communities along the canal.

The Falkirk Wheel
Peter Sandground

The Millennium Link was an ambitious £84.5m project to restore the link between the historic Forth and Clyde and Union Canals, and to provide a corridor of regenerative activity through central Scotland. The major challenge was how to link the Forth and Clyde Canal, which lay 115 feet below the level of the Union Canal. Historically, the two canals had been joined at Falkirk by a flight of eleven locks that stepped down across a distance of nearly a mile, but these had been dismantled in 1933. British Waterways (now Scottish Canals) was keen to present a visionary solution by taking full advantage of the opportunity to create a truly spectacular and fitting structure that would suitably commemorate the Millennium and act as an iconic symbol for years to come. The result was a perfectly balanced structure that is The Falkirk Wheel – the world's first and only rotating boat lift. Completion of The Millennium Link project was officially marked by Her Majesty The Queen on 24 May 2002 at The Falkirk Wheel.

Notes

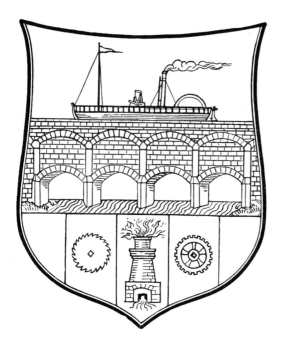

The Coat of Arms of the Burgh of Maryhill
Glasgow Museums and Libraries Collections

Probably designed in 1885, the arms feature a steamship on the Kelvin Aqueduct. Local industries are represented at the base of the shield.

OVERVIEW PP.7–9

1. *Glasgow Herald*, 22 March 1956, p.9.

2. Bowes 1958, pp.63–5.

3. Scott Wilson Kirkpatrick, 1975. The motorway project and an alternative expressway proposal were eventually abandoned by Strathclyde Regional Council in the late 1970s.

INTRODUCTION PP.12–29

1. Redmount 1995, p.135.

2. Biblioteca Ambrosiana. Milano: Leonardo da Vinci, Codex Atlanticus, f. 656a-r.

3. Statistical 1791–9, vol.4, p.543.

4. RCAHMS, CANMORE database entry for Largo Canal.

5. A.L. Prasuhn in Fleming 2000, p.146.

6. Knox 1784, vol.II, p.401.

7. *Encyclopaedia Britannica* 1824, p.484. For Thomas Telford's similarly bleak picture of the state of Scotland's roads in the eighteenth century see Smiles 1867, p.54.

8. National Records of Scotland, ref. GD18/4736. Adam also mentions the opening of the Newry Canal in Ireland, the first summit level canal in the British Isles.

9. Brewster 1830, vol.14, p.249.

10. Graham 1968, pp.170–8 and plates 16–19; Lindsay 1968, pp.99–112; RCAHMS linear description.

11. Lindsay 1968, pp.86–98.

12. Muirhead 1858, p.213.

13. Lindsay 1968, pp.211–15; www.rcahms.gov.uk CANMORE entries.

14. Lindsay 1968, pp178–94.

15. Muirhead 1858, pp.210–11. Alum was used in the production of fabric dyes.

16. Stevenson 1878, p.111; Skempton 2002, p.780; DNB 2004–14, 'John Rennie' entry by Roland Paxton.

17. *Journals of the House of Commons*, vol.62, 9 April 1807, p.313.

18. Pratt 1922, pp.181–241.

19. Paterson 2006, pp.124–32.

20. Select Committee 1839, pp.209–10.

21. Lindsay 1968, p.221.

22. Paterson 2006, p.174.

23. See individual canal entries in Priestley 1831 for relevant legislation and amending legislation.

24. Thomas Telford quoted in Cameron 2005, p.41.

25. *Caledonian Mercury*, 19 August 1769, p.2.

26. Stevenson 1817A, p.500.

27. Smiles 1867, p.232; Paxton and Shipway 2007A, pp.156–7.

28. *Caledonian Mercury*, 31 July 1790, p.3.

29. Paxton and Shipway 2007b, p.252.

30. Stevenson 1817a, pp.499–500.

31. Lindsay 1968, p.39.

32. Groome 1885, vol.II, p.52.

FORTH AND CLYDE CANAL PP.30–43

1. Defoe 1724, vol.III, pp.81–2.

2. Lindsay 1968, p.212.

3. *Caledonian Mercury*, 31 July 1790, p.3; Priestley 1831, pp.266–7.

4. Knox 1784, vol.II, p.401.

5. Vasey 1992, pp.373–377; Ruddock 2002, p.4.

6. Vasey 1992, p.374; Ruddock 2002, p.4.

7. National Records of Scotland, ref. GD18/5023/3/36 (letter from Alexander Gordon to Sir John Clerk of Penicuik, 24 September 1726).

8. National Records of Scotland, ref. GD18/4736a (letter from William Adam to Sir John Clerk of Penicuik, 6 October 1741).

9. Lindsay 1968, p.16.

10. Lindsay 1968, p.16.

11. Priestley 1831, p.267.

12. Cleland 1816, pp.299–300.

13. Smeaton 1797, p.354.

14. *Caledonian Mercury*, 18 June 1768, p.3.

15. *Scots Magazine*, 1 February 1770, p.110.

16. *Scots Magazine*, 1 February 1770, p.110.

17. *Scots Magazine*, 6 July 1772, p.397.

18. Dowds 2003, pp.49–53.

19. *Caledonian Mercury*, 21 June 1787, p.3 (foundation ceremony of the Kelvin Aqueduct).

20. Inscription on the foundation stone.

21. *Caledonian Mercury*, 31 July 1790, p.3.

22. Pratt 1922, p.115.

23. Brewster 1830, American edition vol.14, p.304.

24. Pratt 1922, p.122 (passengers); Lindsay 1968, p.220 (goods); Brewster 1830, American edition vol.14, p.304 (revenue).

25. Pratt 1922, p.132.

26. Paterson 2006, p.199.

27. Abercrombie and Matthew 1946.

28. Lindsay 1968, pp.50–1.

29. IWAAC 1974, pp.1–11.

30. Strathclyde Regional Council's Regional Plan of 1976, cited by J.M. Stirling in Fleming 2000, p.8.

31. Paterson 2006, p.151.

32. See Fleming 2000.

33. *The Herald*, 26 May 2001, p.23.

34. *British Waterways Annual Report and Accounts, 2006–7*, p.23 (new canal link).

35. *British Waterways Annual Report and Accounts, 2003–4*, p.41.

MONKLAND CANAL
PP.44–57

1. Quoted in Muirhead 1858, pp.202–3.

2. Lumsden 1934, pp.452–3.

3. Watt 1770b, pp.1–12.

4. Renwick 1912, p.315.

5. Thomson 1950, p.123.

6. Priestley 1831, p.481.

7. *Scots Magazine*, 1 June 1770, p.340.

8. *Caledonian Mercury*, 7 September 1771, p.2.

9. Letter from James Watt to Dr William Small, 21 November 1772, quoted in Muirhead 1858, p.202.

10. *Aberdeen Journal*, 7 September 1772.

11. Watt 1770a, letter from James Watt to Dr William Small, 7 November 1772.

12. *Caledonian Mercury*, 23 June 1781, p.4.

13. *Morning Herald & Daily Advertiser*, 23 October 1784, p.3.

14. *Public Advertiser*, 23 August 1793, p.2 (first boats through the locks on 22 August 1793).

15. Cleland 1816, vol.I, p.313.

16. Cleland 1816, vol.I, p.313; Pratt 1922, pp.147–8; Lindsay 1968, p.59.

17. Groome 1885, vol.III, p.45.

18. Pratt 1922, pp.149–50; Lindsay 1968, p.61.

19. Pratt 1922, p.154.

20. *Warrant of Abandonment: Monkland Canal*, 28 August 1950.

21. For numerous post-war parliamentary questions about accidents at the Monkland Canal see *Hansard* (http://hansard. millbanksystems.com), for example vol.522, cc29–30W, 15 December 1953 for the 1951–3 child drowning accident figures.

22. *Sunday Post*, 2 September 1945, p.3.

23. Abercrombie and Matthew 1946, p.238.

CRINAN CANAL PP.58–69

1. Knox 1784, vol.II, pp.412–6.

2. RCAHMS 1992, pp.506–9.

3. National Records of Scotland, ref. GD18/5023/6.

4. Birmingham Central Library, James Watt Papers, ref. JWP 4/62 and 4/82. The Board for the Forfeited Annexed Estates was established in 1752 to manage the forfeited estates that were annexed to the Crown following the suppression of the 1745 Jacobite Rising. Under the 1752 Annexing Act, the rents and profits from the annexed estates were intended 'for the better civilising and improvement of the Highlands of Scotland; and preventing Disorders there for the future'.

5. See Anderson 1785, pp.395–402 and Knox 1784, vol. II, pp.412–6.

6. Select Committee 1839, p.204; *The London Gazette*, 21 August 1792, p.656.

7. Select Committee 1839, pp.203–6 (transcription of 1792 Crinan Canal Prospectus).

8. Select Committee 1839, pp.203–6 (transcription of 1792 Crinan Canal Prospectus); *Caledonian Mercury*, 26 November 1792, p.4.

9. Select Committee 1839, p.208.

10. *Caledonian Mercury*, 22 February 1798, p.2.

11. *Caledonian Mercury*, 5 December 1793, p.1 (advertisement for timber issued by the canal office at Inveraray); *Scots Magazine*, 10 February 1795, vol.LVI, p.vi (30 June 1794, digging of the Crinan Canal commenced); Lindsay 1968, p119 (steam-engine).

12. For example see *Caledonian Mercury*, 13 October 1794, p.1 (advertisement for a masonry contract to build a pier at Ardrishaig, a large culvert and smaller pieces of masonry work); *Caledonian Mercury*, 9 January 1794, p.1 (advertisement for timber contractors, who were advised to send proposals to Rennie at Stamford Street, London, or to the canal company's clerk, Humphrey Graham, at Inveraray); *Caledonian Mercury*, 4 July 1795, p.1 (advertisement for masonry contractors to build the sea lock at Crinan);

13. *Caledonian Mercury*, 28 February 1799, p.3 (defaulting subscribers); *Caledonian Mercury*, 25 May 1799, p.1 (advertisement for contractors to complete the remaining five locks).

14. *Journals of the House of Commons*, vol.54, pp.646

(14 June 1799), 678 (21 June 1799, and 693 (25 June 1799).

15. Cross-Rudkin 2010, p.37.

16. *Glasgow Journal*, 28 July 1801.

17. *Caledonian Mercury*, 31 August 1809, p.3.

18. Pratt 1922, p.63.

19. Lindsay 1968, p.129.

20. Pratt 1922, p.66.

21. Pratt 1922, pp.75–90.

22. *British Waterways Annual Report and Accounts, 2009–10*, p.20.

CALEDONIAN CANAL PP.70–87

1. Burt 1754, vol. 2, Letter XXVI (about 1737), pp.335–6.

2. Mackenzie 1878, p.4.

3. Watt 1774. The Commission of Police was established in 1714 to exercise various aspects of Crown patronage in Scotland, and came to make recommendations to the government in London on numerous other matters, including 'pacification' of the Highlands after the Jacobite risings, maintaining the poor, river navigations and repairing the roads. The sinecure was abolished in 1782.

4. Telford 1803; Telford 1838, pp.290–301.

5. Priestley 1831, pp.126–7. The first commissioners were the Speaker of the House of Commons, the Chancellor of the Exchequer and the Master of the Rolls.

6. Burton 1999, pp.75–82.

7. Smiles 1867, pp.232–3.

8. Cameron 2005, p.27.

9. *Caledonian Mercury*, 22 July 1805, p.4.

10. *Scots Magazine*, February 1909, p.101 ('A Journey through the Highlands and Western Isles, in the Summer of 1804 – In a Series of Letters to a Friend'; Letter VIII by the Ettrick Shepherd).

11. *Caledonian Mercury*, 22 July 1805, p.4.

12. *Hansard*, vol.19, 3 May 1811, cc.786–7.

13. Ross 1888, pp.333–4.

14. Telford 1838, p.55 (note).

15. *Caledonian Mercury*, 28 October 1822, p.3.

16. Pratt 1922, p.17.

17. Burton 1999, p.93.

18. Cameron 2005, p.117. Jackson & Bean of Aston, Birmingham, were the contractors.

19. Lindsay 1968, p.167; Pratt 1922, p.27.

20. *Inverness Courier*, 21 September 1847, pp.2–3.

21. George Ballinger in Paxton 2007, p.9.

22. Bowes 1958, p.63.

23. Cameron 2005, p.146.

24. Cameron 2005, p.173.

25. *British Waterways Annual Report and Accounts, 2006–7*, p.22.

26. *British Waterways Annual Report and Accounts, 2007–8*, p.16.

27. *British Waterways Annual Report and Accounts, 2009–10*, p.19.

UNION CANAL PP.88–101

1. Anonymous 1817a, p.224.

2. See *Caledonian Mercury*, 3 February 1817, p.4, for a letter about the naming of the canal after the objective of uniting the cities of Edinburgh and Glasgow. Unlike Union Street in Aberdeen, for example, the canal was not named in celebration of the Acts of Union of the Kingdom of Great Britain and Kingdom of Ireland in 1800.

3. Lindsay 1968, p.77.

4. *Scots Magazine*, 1 February 1791, p.99; Fraser 1803, pp.99–100.

5. *Caledonian Mercury*, 10 May 1794, p.3.

6. Rennie 1797.

7. Baird 1813.

8. See Anonymous 1817b.

9. *Scots Magazine*, May 1815, pp.337–9 ('Mr Telford's Report on the Union Canal'); Stevenson 1817b.

10. Priestley 1831, p.230.

11. Chapman 1820, p.71.

12. Institution of Civil Engineers, Telford Collection, refs.T/ E G.1–313.

13. Chapman 1820, p.72.

14. *Scots Magazine*, March 1819, p.270; *Caledonian Mercury*, 21 January 1821, p.3.

15. *Caledonian Mercury*, 26 January 1822, p.4.

16. *Aberdeen Journal*, 13 March 1822, p.4.

17. *Glasgow Herald*, 10 May 1822, p.4.

18. Pratt 1922, pp.162-3.

19. Lindsay 1968, p.79.

20. Pratt 1922, pp.167-8.

21. Lindsay 1968, p.84.

22. The sites of locks nine, ten and eleven at Summerford were investigated by Scottish Waterways Trust's Canal College students and Archaeology Scotland in 2014.

23. Hutton 1993a, p.51.

24. Paxton, Stirling and Fleming 2000, pp.67-71.

Bibliography

ABERCROMBIE AND
MATTHEW 1946
Patrick Abercrombie and Robert
Hogg Matthew, *Clyde Valley
Regional Plan 1946*, Edinburgh,
published 1949

AINSLIE AND WHITWORTH
1797
John Ainslie and Robert
Whitworth Jr, *Report of John
Ainslie and Robert Whitworth
jun. concerning the practica-
bility and expence of making
the different tracks proposed
for a canal betwixt the cities
of Edinburgh and Glasgow*,
Edinburgh, 1797 (via Gale
Eighteenth Century Collections
Online, National Library of
Scotland)

ANDERSON 1785
James C. Anderson, *An Account
of the Hebrides and Western
Coasts of Scotland*, Edinburgh,
1785

ANONYMOUS 1767
Anonymous, *Considerations
upon the intended navigable
communication between the
Friths [sic] of Forth and Clyde.
In a letter to the Lord Provost of
Edinburgh, Preses [sic] of the
General Convention of the Royal
Boroughs of Scotland, from
a member of the Convention*,
Edinburgh, 11 April 1767
(via Gale Eighteenth Century
Collections Online, National
Library of Scotland)

ANONYMOUS 1817A
Anonymous, *The Stranger's
Guide to Edinburgh*, Edinburgh,
1817
(via www.books.google.co.uk)

ANONYMOUS 1817B
Anonymous contributors,
*Papers in Opposition to the
Union Canal*, Leith, 1817
(via www.books.google.co.uk)

BAIRD 1813
Hugh Baird, *Report on the
Proposed Edinburgh and
Glasgow Union Canal*,
Edinburgh, 20 September 1813

BOWES 1958
H. Leslie Bowes, *Report of the
Parliamentary Committee of
Inquiry into Inland Waterways*,
London, 1958

BREWSTER 1830
David Brewster (ed.), *The
Edinburgh Encyclopaedia*, 18
vols, Edinburgh and London,
1830
(American edition of 1832 via
www.books.google.co.uk;
'navigation inland', covering
Scotland's canals, is in vol.14)

BRINDLEY, YEOMAN AND
GOLBORNE 1768
James Brindley, Thomas
Yeoman, J. Golborne, *Reports
by James Brindley engineer,
Thomas Yeoman engineer,
and F.R.S. and John Golborne
engineer relative to a Navigable
Communication Betwixt the
Friths of Forth and Clyde*,
Edinburgh, 1768

BROWN 1997
Hamish M. Brown, *Exploring the
Edinburgh to Glasgow Canals
(the Union Canal, the Forth and
Clyde Canal)*, Edinburgh, 1997

BROWN 2010
David H. Brown, 'Scottish
Canal Reservoirs – a historical
perspective' in *Dams and
Reservoirs*, London, 2009 and
2010. 3 parts: Lowlands, vol.19,
issue 3, pp.111–18; Crinan Canal,
vol.19, issue 4, pp.163–70;
Caledonian Canal, vol.20, issue
1, pp.39–43

BURT 1754
Edward Burt, *Letters from
A Gentleman in the North of
Scotland to His Friend in London*,
2 vols, London, 1754

(via Gale Eighteenth Century
Collections Online, National
Library of Scotland)

BURTON 1999
Anthony Burton, *Thomas Telford*,
London, 1999

CAMERON 2005
A. D. Cameron, *The Caledonian
Canal* (4th edition), Edinburgh,
2005

CHAPMAN 1820
Robert Chapman, *The
Topographical Picture of
Glasgow*, Glasgow, 1820
(via www.books.google.co.uk)

CLELAND 1816
James Cleland, *Annals of
Glasgow, comprising an
Account of the Public Buildings,
Charities, and the Rise and
Progress of the City*, 2 vols,
Glasgow, 1816
(via www.openlibrary.org)

COLVIN 1978
Howard Colvin, A *Biographical
Dictionary of British Architects
1600–1840*, London, 1978

CROSS-RUDKIN 2010
Peter Cross-Rudkin, 'Canal
Contractors 1760–1820' in the
*Journal of The Railway and Canal
Historical Society*, vol.36, part 7,
no.207, March 2010, pp.27–39

CUMBERLIDGE 2013
Jane Cumberlidge (compiler),
*Map of the Inland Waterways
of Scotland*, St Ives,
Cambridgeshire, 2013

DEFOE 1724
Daniel Defoe, *A tour thro' the
whole island of Great Britain,
Divided into Circuits or Journies*,
3 vols, London, 1724
(via Gale Eighteenth Century
Collections Online, National
Library of Scotland)

DICKINSON 1935
Henry Winram Dickinson, *James Watt: Craftsman & Engineer*, Cambridge, 1935

DNB 2004–14
Oxford Dictionary of National Biography
(via www.oxforddnb.com)

DOWDS 2003
T.J. Dowds, *The Forth and Clyde Canal: A History*, East Linton, 2003

ENCYCLOPAEDIA BRITANNICA 1824
Supplement to the 4th, 5th and 6th Editions of the Encyclopaedia Britannica, vol.6, Edinburgh, 1824
(via Google Books: www.books.google.com)

FLEMING 2000
George Fleming (ed.), *The Millennium Link: the Rehabilitation of the Forth and Clyde and Union Canals*, London, 2000

FRASER 1803
Robert Fraser, *A Letter to the Rt. Hon. Charles Abbot, Speaker of the House of Commons, Containing an Inquiry into the Most Effectual Means of the Improvement of the Coasts and Western Isles of Scotland, and the Extension of the Fisheries*, London, 1803
(via Google Books: www.books.google.com)

GRAHAM 1968
Angus Graham, 'Two Canals in Aberdeenshire' in *Proceedings of the Society of Antiquaries of Scotland*, vol.100, Edinburgh, 1968, pp.170–8
(via www.archaeologydataservice.ac.uk)

GROOME 1885
Francis Groome, *Ordnance Gazetteer of Scotland*, 5 vols, Edinburgh, 1885
(via www.openlibrary.org)

HADFIELD 1993
Charles Hadfield, *Thomas Telford's Temptation: Telford and William Jessop's Reputation*, Cleobury Mortimer, 1993

HADFIELD AND SKEMPTON 1979
Charles Hadfield and Alec W. Skempton, *William Jessop, Engineer*, Newton Abbot, 1979

HALDANE 1962
Archibald Richard Burdon Haldane, *New Ways through the Glens; Highland Road, Bridge and Canal Makers of the Early 19th Century*, London, 1962

HOPKIRK 1816
James Hopkirk, *Account of the Forth and Clyde Canal Navigation from its Origin to the Present Time*, Glasgow, 1816

HOWAT 2002
John M.T. Howat, 'Sir Andrew Wood's Canal' in *Industrial Heritage*, vol.28, no.2, summer 2002, pp. 21–3

HUME 1976
John Hume, *The Industrial Archaeology of Scotland*, 2 vols, London, 1976

HUTTON 1991
Guthrie Hutton, *A Forth and Clyde Canalbum*, Glasgow, 1991

HUTTON 1992
Guthrie Hutton, *Caledonian Canal: the Monster Canal*, Glasgow, 1992

HUTTON 1993A
Guthrie Hutton, *The Union Canal: A Capital Asset*, Glasgow, 1993

HUTTON 1993B
Guthrie Hutton, *Monkland: the Canal that made Money*, Ochiltree, 1993

HUTTON 1994
Guthrie Hutton, *The Crinan Canal: Puffers and Paddle Steamers*, Ochiltree, 1994

HUTTON 2002
Guthrie Hutton, *Scotland's Millennium Canals: the Survival and Revival of the Forth and Clyde and Union Canals*, Catrine, 2002

IWAAC 1974
Inland Waterways Amenity Advisory Council, *Scottish Waterways: Forth and Clyde Canal; Union Canal – A Report to the Secretary of State for the Environment*, London, October 1974
(via www.waterways.org.uk)

KNOX 1784
John Knox, *A View of the British Empire, more especially Scotland; with some Proposals for the Improvement of that Country, the Extension of its Fisheries, and the Relief of the People*, 2 vols, London, 1784

(3rd edition, via www.openlibrary.org)

LARKIN 1819
Larkin, *Sketch of a tour in the Highlands of Scotland; through Perthshire, Argyleshire, and Inverness-shire, in September and October, 1818; with some account of the Caledonian Canal*, London, 1819
(via www.books.google.co.uk)

LINDSAY 1968
Jean Lindsay, *The Canals of Scotland*, Newton Abbott, 1968

LINDSAY 2012
Jean Lindsay, 'The Forth and Clyde Canal – Conflict and its Motto' in *Journal of the Railway Canal Historical Society*, no. 215, November 2012

LUMSDEN 1934
Harry Lumsden, *Records of the Trades House of Glasgow, 1713–1777*, Edinburgh, 1934

MACDOUGALL 1976
Lesley MacDougall, *The Crinan Canal: An Illustrated History and Guide*, Alexandria, 1976

MACKELL 1767
Robert Mackell, *An account of the navigable canal, proposed to be cut from the river Clyde to the river Carron, as surveyed by Robert Mackell and James Watt*, London, 1767
(via Gale Eighteenth Century Collections Online, National Library of Scotland)

MACKENZIE 1878
Alexander Mackenzie, *Prophecies of the Brahan Seer*, Inverness, 1878
(via www.openlibrary.org)

MASSIE 1989
Edward Massie, 'The Aberdeenshire Canal' in *Transactions of the Buchan Field Club*, vol.XVIII, 1989, p.45

MUIRHEAD 1858
James Patrick Muirhead, *The Life of James Watt with Selections from his Correspondence*, London, 1858

PATERSON 2006
Len Paterson, *From Sea to Sea: A History of the Scottish Lowland and Highland Canals*, Glasgow, 2006

PAXTON 2007
Roland Paxton (ed.), *The 250th Anniversary of the Birth of Thomas Telford* (The Royal

Society of Edinburgh conference papers), Edinburgh, 2007

PAXTON AND SHIPWAY 2007A
Roland Paxton and Jim Shipway, *Civil Engineering Heritage: Scotland – Highlands and Islands*, London, 2007

PAXTON AND SHIPWAY 2007B
Roland Paxton and Jim Shipway, *Civil Engineering Heritage: Scotland – Lowlands and Borders*, London, 2007

PAXTON, STIRLING AND FLEMING 2000
Roland Paxton, Jim Stirling and George Fleming, 'Regeneration of the Forth and Clyde and Union Canals' in *Proceedings of ICE – Civil Engineering*, vol.138, issue 2, London, 1 May 2000, pp.61–72

PEARSON 1986
David Pearson, 'The Aberdeenshire Canal: a description and Interpretation of its Remains' in *Aberdeen University Review*, vol.51, spring 1986, p.285

PEARSON 2011
David Pearson, 'The Aberdeenshire Canal up to 1810' in *Journal of the Railway Canal Historical Society*, no.211, 2011

PENFOLD 1980
Alastair Penfold, 'Managerial organization on the Caledonian Canal' in

PHILIPS 1792
John Phillips, *A General History of Inland Navigation, Foreign and Domestic*

Containing a Complete Account of the Canals Already Executed in England with Considerations on those Projected, London, 1792

(4th edition of 1803 via www.openlibrary.org)

PRATT 1922
Edwin A. Pratt, *Scottish Canals and Waterways comprising State Canals, Railway-owned Canals and Present-Day Ship Canal Schemes*, London, 1922
(via www.openlibrary.org)

PRIESTLEY 1831
Joseph Priestley, *Historical Account of the Navigable Rivers, Canals, and Railways, of Great Britain*, London, 1831
(via www.openlibrary.org)

RACKWITZ 2007
Martin Rackwitz, *Travels to Terra Incognita: The Scottish Highlands and Hebrides in Early Modern Travellers' Accounts circa 1600 to 1800*, Münster, 2007

RANSOM 1999
P.J.G. Ransom, *Scotland's Inland Waterways: Canals, Rivers and Lochs*, Edinburgh, 1999

RCAHMS 1992
RCAHMS, *ARGYLL: AN INVENTORY OF THE MONUMENTS – MID ARGYLL & COWAL: MEDIEVAL & LATER MONUMENTS*, VOL.7, EDINBURGH, 1992, PP.506–10 (via www.scotlandsplaces.gov.uk)

REDMOUNT 1995
Carol A. Redmount, 'The Wadi Tumilat and the "Canal of the Pharoahs"' in *Journal of Near Eastern Studies*, vol.54, no.2, Chicago, April 1995, pp.127–35

RENNIE 1797
John Rennie, *Report concerning the different lines surveyed by Messrs. John Ainslie & Robert Whitworth, Jun. for a canal, proposed to be made between the cities of Edinburgh and Glasgow, and intended to communicate with the Frith of Forth at Leith, and the River Clyde at the Broomie Law; with an account of a running level, taken for a new line by Linlithgow and Falkirk*, Edinburgh, 14 September 1797

RENWICK 1912
Robert Renwick, *Extracts from the Records of the Burgh of Glasgow with Charters and Other Documents, 1760–80*, vol. VII, Glasgow, 1912

ROSS 1888
Alexander Ross, 'Notes on the Formation of the Caledonian Canal, and its Effects on the Highlands' in *Transactions of the Gaelic Society of Inverness*, vol. XIII (1886–7), Inverness, 1888, pp.313–34 (via www.openlibrary.org)

ROYAL COMMISSION 1906
Royal Commission on Canals and Inland Navigations of the United Kingdom, *Reports and Minutes of Evidence*, London, 1906–11

RUDDOCK 1979
Ted Ruddock, *Arch Bridges and their Builders 1735–1835*, Cambridge, 1979

RUDDOCK 2002
Ted Ruddock, 'John Adair' in *Biographical Dictionary of Civil Engineers* (ed. Alec Skempton), vol.1, London, 2002

SCOTT WILSON KIRKPATRICK 1975
Scott Wilson Kirkpatrick, *Maryhill Motorway*, Glasgow, May 1975

SELECT COMMITTEE 1839
House of Commons, *Report from the Select Committee on the Caledonian and Crinan Canals*, London, 1839 (via www.books.google.co.uk)

SKEMPTON 2002
Alec W. Skempton (ed.), *A Biographical Dictionary of Civil Engineers in Great Britain*, London, 2002

SMEATON 1767
John Smeaton, *The report of John Smeaton Engineer, and F. R. S. concerning The Practicability and Expence of joining the Rivers Forth and Clyde by a Navigable Canal, and thereby to join the East Sea and the West*, Edinburgh, 1767 (via Gale Eighteenth Century Collections Online, National Library of Scotland)

SMEATON 1797
John Smeaton, *Reports of the Late Mr. John Smeaton, F.R.S. Made on various occasions in the course of his employment of an engineer*, London, 1797 (via Gale Eighteenth Century Collections Online, National Library of Scotland)

SMILES 1867
Samuel Smiles, *The Life of Thomas Telford, Civil Engineer, with an Introductory History of Roads and Travelling in Great Britain*, London, 1867 (via www.openlibrary.org)

SMITH 1776
Adam Smith, *An Inquiry into the Causes and Nature of the Wealth of Nations*, 2 vols, London, 1776 (via Gale Eighteenth Century Collections Online, National Library of Scotland)

STATISTICAL 1791–9
Various authors, *First (Old) Statistical Account*, Edinburgh, 1791–9 (via www.edina.ac.uk/stat-acc-scot/)

STEVENSON 1817A
Robert Stevenson, 'General View of the Works executed on the Line of the Caledonian Canal' in *The Scots Magazine*, July 1817, pp.497–508 (quoted from the 1817 Supplement to the *Encyclopaedia Britannica*, vol. II, part II) (via www.books.google.co.uk)

STEVENSON 1817B
Robert Stevenson, *Report relative to a line of canal upon one level between the cities of Edinburgh and Glasgow, to form a junction with the Forth and Clyde Canal at Lock No. 20 and also with the Port of Leith, and the Broomielaw at Glasgow*, Edinburgh, 1817

STEVENSON 1878
David Stevenson, *Life of Robert Stevenson*, Edinburgh, 1878 (via www.openlibrary.org)

TELFORD 1803
Thomas Telford, *Survey and Report of the Coasts and Central Highlands of Scotlan;, made by the Command of the Right Honourable the Lords Commissioners of His Majesty's Treasury, in the Autumn of 1802*, London, 1803 (text printed in Telford 1838, Appendix B, pp.290–301)

TELFORD 1838
Thomas Telford, John Rickman (ed.), *Life of Thomas Telford, Civil Engineer, Written By Himself*, London, 1838 (via www.books.google.co.uk)

THOMSON 1950
George Thomson, 'James Watt and the Monkland Canal' in *The Scottish Historical Review*, vol. XXIX, no.108, Edinburgh, October 1950, pp.121–33

VASEY 1992
Peter G. Vasey, 'The Forth-Clyde Canal: John Adair, Progenitor of Early Schemes' in *Journal of the Railway Canal Historical Society*, vol. XXX, pt.7, no.150, March 1992, pp.373–7

WATT 1770A
Birmingham Central Library, *Industrial Revolution: a Documentary History – the Boulton and Watt Archive and the Matthew Boulton papers from the Birmingham Central Library, Muirhead I Collection*, series 1, part 2, Marlborough, 1993 (microform via Adam Matthew Publications)

WATT 1770B
James Watt, *A Scheme for making a Navigable Canal from the City of Glasgow to the Monkland Coalierys*, Glasgow, 1770 (via Gale Eighteenth Century Collections Online, National Library of Scotland)

WATT 1774
James Watt, 'Appendix No.22: Mr Watt's Survey, Report and Estimate [for a canal between Inverness and Fort William]' of March 1774 in *First report from the Committee Appointed to Enquire into the State of the British Fisheries*, London, 11 May 1785 (via www.books.google.co.uk)

WHITWORTH 1785
Robert Whitworth, *Report of Robert Whitworth, Esq., engineer to the Company of Proprietors of the Forth and Clyde Navigation, relative to the tract of the intended canal, from Stockingfield Westward, and different places of entry into the River Clyde, with estimates of the expence of finishing the same, to Fluckhole – to Dalnotter – and to Bowling Bay. Referring to a plan and profile of the canal with a survey of the River Clyde, and soundings thereof, from Fluckhole to Dunglass Castle. And pointing out where several additional supplies of water may be got, sufficient for every purpose of the navigation*, Edinburgh, 1785 (via Gale Eighteenth Century Collections Online, National Library of Scotland)

MANUSCRIPT COLLECTIONS

Argyll and Bute Council Archives
Birmingham Central Library (James Watt papers)
East Dunbartonshire Archives and Local Studies
Edinburgh City Archives
Falkirk Museums and Archives
Glasgow City Archives, Mitchell Library
Highland Archive Service
Institution of Civil Engineers, London (Thomas Telford papers)
National Archives, Kew, London (British Waterways records)
National Library of Scotland, Edinburgh (John Rennie and Thomas Telford papers)
National Records of Scotland, Edinburgh
North Lanarkshire Archives
Parliamentary Archives, Palace of Westminster, London (bills, acts and associated papers)
The Royal Society (Smeaton drawings)
Scottish Canals Archive, Glasgow
West Dunbartonshire Council Archives
West Lothian Council Archives and Records

ONLINE RESOURCES

Aberdeen City Libraries: www.silvercityvault.org.uk
Am Baile (Highland History & Culture): www.ambaile.org.uk
British Library: www.bl.uk
British Newspaper Archive*: www.britishnewspaperarchive.co.uk
Capital Collections (City of Edinburgh): www.capitalcollections.org.uk
Dictionary of Scottish Architects: www.scottisharchitects.org.uk
Falkirk Museums and Archives: http://collections.falkirk.gov.uk/home.page.do
The Glasgow Story: www.theglasgowstory.com
Google Books: www.books.google.co.uk
Historic Scotland: www.historic-scotland.gov.uk
Inland Waterways Association: www.waterways.org.uk
Internet Archive (full text publications): www.archive.org
JSTOR* (full text journals): www.jstor.org
National Library of Scotland: www.nls.uk
National Museums of Scotland: www.nms.ac.uk
National Records of Scotland: www.nrscotland.gov.uk
Royal Commission on the Ancient and Historical Monuments of Scotland (RCAHMS): www.rcahms.gov.uk
Scottish Archive Network: www.scan.org.uk
Scottish Canals: www.scottishcanals.co.uk
Scottish Cultural Resources Access Network (SCRAN)*: www.scran.ac.uk
Scotland's Places: www.scotlandsplaces.gov.uk
Scottish Waterways Trust: www.scottishwaterwaystrust.org.uk
Virtual Mitchell (Mitchell Library, Glasgow): www.mitchelllibrary.org/virtualmitchell
Virtual Waterways (online archive for British Waterways): www.virtualwaterways.co.uk
* Subscription may be required.

COPYRIGHT CREDITS

The publisher gratefully acknowledges the following individuals and organisations who have contributed photographic material to this book.

Page 40 by kind permission of Alexander Duncan Bell, Architectural Illustrator, Edinburgh; pages 26, 27 and 38 © Falkirk Archives; pages 8, 27 and 102 © CSG CIC Glasgow Museums and Libraries Collections; pages 16–17, 18 © Glasgow University Archives Service; pages 19, 37 and 50 © Glasgow University Library, Special Collections; back cover and pages 15, 21, 23, 24, 30–1, 41, 42, 55, 56, 57, 77, 80, 81 and 84 © Nick Haynes; pages 28–9 © Inverness Museum and Art Gallery; pages 12-13 © Jorisvo/IStock; page 32 courtesy of the Trustees of the National Library of Scotland, Edinburgh; page 74 courtesy National Museums, Liverpool; page 35 © National Portrait Gallery, London; page 19 (DP 015172), page 20 (SC 790832), page 22 (SC 681830), page 25 (SC 387235, Sir William Arrol Collection), page 51 (SC 1257612), page 52 (SC 646182, image reproduced courtesy of J.R. Hume), page 53 (000-000-117-569c, licensor SCRAN), page 53 (SC 586791 and SC 586793, images reproduced courtesy of J.R. Hume), page 54 (DP 032105), page 60 (DP 032083), page 63 (DP 157160 and DP 157171, J.B. Mackenzie Photograph Albums vol.1), page 64 (SC 791280, image reproduced courtesy of J.R. Hume), page 76 (SC 350351 and SC 549313, images reproduced courtesy of J.R. Hume), page 78 (DP 025501), page 79 (DP 023911), page 91 (SC 700208), page 91 (SC 785646, Francis M. Chrystal Collection), page 92 (SC 409294, Francis M. Chrystal Collection), page 92 (SC 677855, image reproduced courtesy of J.R. Hume), page 93 (SC 409289 and SC 677924, Francis M. Chrystal Collection), page 93 (SC 1071699, image reproduced courtesy of Edinburgh Photographic Society), page 94 (SC 409292 and SC 409290, Francis M. Chrystal Collection) and page 95 (SC 677929, Francis M. Chrystal Collection), all © RCAHMS; page 35 © Royal Society, London; front cover, frontispiece and pages 23, 42, 43, 64, 65, 66, 67, 68, 69, 81, 82, 83, 85, 86-7, 90, 95, 96, 97, 98, 99, 100 and 101 © Peter Sandground; pages 6, 14 and 36 © Science Museum/Science & Society Picture Library; pages 33, 46-7, 49 and 72-3 © Scottish Canals; pages 48 and 61 © Scottish National Portrait Gallery, Edinburgh; pages 44–5 © Keith Fergus, pages 58-9 © D. Habron, pages 70-1 © D.Houghton and pages 88-9 © Simon Williams, all Scottish Viewpoint; page 17 © Scottish Life Archive (000-000-569-620-R), page 39 © Scotsman Publications Ltd (000-000-043-872-R), page 39 © Newsquest (Herald & Times) (000-000-117-624-C) and page 53 © Newsquest (Herald & Times) (000-000-117-569-C), licensor SCRAN; page 36 courtesy of the Trustees of Sir John Soane's Museum, photo Ardon Bar-Hama.